A Dialectical Perspective on the Concept of Romanticism: Multiple Ideologies in an Infinitely Expanding Framework

A Dialectical Perspective on the Concept of Romanticism: Multiple Ideologies in an Infinitely Expanding Framework

By Nicklas Skovgaard Petersen

BoD

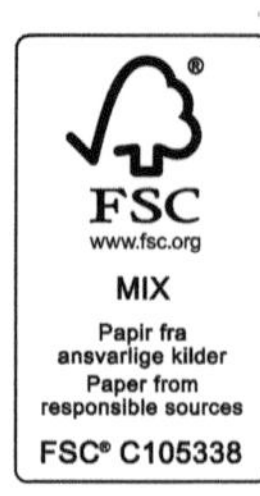

Publisher: BoD – Copenhagen, Denmark

Printing: BoD – Norderstedt, Germany

ISBN: 9788743013563

Contents

Summary

The concept of Romanticism has undergone a complete reinvigoration in recent literary history. This is because new ideas and perspectives have made it possible to include additional cultural theory to the canon of works which has called for complete alteration of emphasis placed on traditional values related to the concept. In the following, I argue for a dialectical approach that is able to accommodate new information as part of the Romantic framework. This is important because past studies on the subject have deliberately sought to define the concept based on a presupposed canon of works. Such an orderly and narrow approach can only represent fragments of the past because it does not take into account the surrounding cultural context and is not open to new information that might call for a change of emphasis. The Romantic period is precisely characterised by sharp cultural conflict and vast differences between the Romantic writers so it is fragmentary to define the concept based solely on their similarities.

In a dialectical approach, opposing artists to the Romantic position will instead of being pushed outside the framework take the form of an antithesis. This process creates a philosophical forum. In the forum, the thesis of the traditional conception of truth and its antithesis generate a synthesis. Every new piece of information provided by literary historians and critics either contributes to the dynamic of the framework or expands it. This is because information on canonical writers contributes to the overall knowledge of their position within the framework in relation to the other writers. Information on new writers or genres might also provide cause for including it in the literary canon and thus it provides cause for change in the general consensus of the concept. A dialectical approach to the study of literary history is therefore very important because it steps beyond the limitations of theoretical forms and thus provides a much more rounded representation of the past which ultimately affects many areas of literary and cultural theory.

The paper consists of four chapters. In the first chapter, I discuss the renowned scholar Jerome McGann's essay "Rethinking Romanticism" from 1996 in which he argues for the possibilities of a rethinking of the concept. I analyse and compare it to the orderly approach offered by the literary intellectual René Wellek in 1949 from his famous work "The Concept of Romanticism in Literary History". On the background of an examination on the evolution of the concept of Romanticism I argue that McGann's approach offers a more plausible representation of the past than Wellek's theory because it is built on a free idea of the concept and thus it can accommodate a much broader synthesis.

In Chapters 2 and 3, I analyse and compare two of the arguably greatest and most influential epics of the time, William Wordsworth's *The Prelude* and Lord Byron's *Don Juan*. Wellek argues that a specific perspective on the three central elements of imagination, nature and symbol makes up the core of the concept. In this light, Wellek's synthesis solely accommodates the ideology of the Lake Poets while the ideologies of other writers which do not share the same ideas such as Byron's ideology are pushed to the periphery of the framework. However in a dialectical framework, the ideology of Byron takes the form of an antithesis to the Romantic position and thus the ideologies of Wordsworth and Byron generate a synthesis within a larger philosophical forum.

Chapter 4 discusses in which direction the expanding framework is headed. As the dialectical framework is expanding, it opens up for additional cultural theory to be included in Romantic literary research. New areas of canonicity are therefore explored which results in the inclusion of additional contexts, genres, themes and writers as parts of the Romantic canon. In this context, I argue that the inclusion of feministic and gender-based theory especially challenge the traditionally male dominated canon of works. I focus on the life and works of the famous actress and poet Mary Robinson. I analyse and discuss her original poems "January 1795", "Winkfield Plain" and "The Haunted Beach" as well as her poetic exchange with Samuel Taylor Coleridge which resulted in such remarkable poems such as "Ode, Inscribed to the

Infant Son of ST Coleridge" and "Mrs. Robinson to the poet Coleridge". Her original poetic contributions and her active involvement with the Lake Poets during the literary revolution mean that she has earned her place as a Romantic poet within the framework of Romanticism.

A Plausible Perspective

This is a paper that focuses on past and present literary history. It discusses the fundamental problems that arise when solely thinking in terms of classifications. It furthermore provides an alternative to this line of thinking. It discusses a way to step beyond the limitations of theoretical forms. These forms are understandable however, since human beings are accustomed to thinking in categories and classifications. They serve many practical purposes, not least within the realm of literary history. Literary classifications have proven useful to get an overview of certain subjects in order to further the understanding of works of a specific time and thereby expand the platform for further study. The literary scholar David Perkins discusses in his work *Is Literary History Possible?* from 1992, whether literary history as a discipline can represent the past with acceptable clarity. The answer is that it cannot, but it is equally evident that it is a necessary discipline. It is necessary to visualise the past because it helps shape the cultural mentality of the present. He explains that the discipline of literary history became intellectually profound in the eighteenth century and is founded on the ideas of many major modes of literary and cultural theory. By the time of the nineteenth century literary history was classified by three fundamental assumptions: "that literary works are formed by their historical context; that change in literature takes place developmentally; and that this change is the unfolding of an idea, principle, or suprapersonal entity" (Perkins, p. 1-2) This orderly viewpoint has then proved incomplete because for postmodern literary historians this constructed line of thinking can only represent incoherent fragments of the past, and thus does not offer a plausible perspective. It is such a plausible perspective that this paper aims to present. It seeks to present a perspective that places a wider frame in its representation of the past and thus present a more rounded conception of truth.

My aim is to look beyond the literary framework and further the understanding of the development of a dialectical philology that is not bound by its theoretical forms. This is further explained by the renowned American scholar Jerome McGann who states that the theory is not to be viewed as a conceptual structure, but instead as a "set of investigative practices, and a set of practices that play themselves out under a horizon of falsiability" (McGann, p. 165). This theory is important because it aims to develop the study of literary history to go beyond the labelling of literary classifications. It will instead base further study on ideas that are free of any empirical basis with a focus on the dynamic internal relationships and cultural differences of literary movements rather than simply focus on the similarities of a presupposed canon of works. The objective is then to create a consensus of a "current world-historical perspective" (McGann, p. 166) that will allow for radical and alternative study and changes of emphases in literary critique.

This dialectical philology bases itself on Hegel's formulation of the dialectic. When a theorist pursues a claim of truth, he produces a thesis. This is then countered by another writer who produces an argument to rival the current thesis. This counter-argument then generates its antithesis. The thesis and the antithesis then produce a discourse of philosophical argument. This contradictory process then produces a more rounded viewpoint of both sides within a larger framework. It produces a synthesis. This viewpoint is then countered by another antithesis which goes into the framework and broadens the synthesis. I will align this process with the writings of the Romantic Movement. This is because through the twentieth century the synthesis of the ideologies of the Lake School poets has been central to the dominant literary historical perspective of the Romantic period. This is while its antithesis has been moved to the periphery of literary theory. This is apparent since a literary perspective that generalises the concept based on a presupposed set of criteria is too narrow to fit a broader synthesis.

I will therefore argue for an understanding of Romanticism that can accommodate not only a broader synthesis, but an infinitely expanding synthesis of the concept. I will argue that there is no ideology that stands as central to the understanding of the concept. There are however, multiple ideologies that stand as equally contributing to the dynamic of a constantly expanding framework. I will analyse the ideology of the arguably greatest poet of the age William Wordsworth and his masterpiece *The Prelude* with a focus on the poet's attitude towards the normative Romantic elements of nature, imagination, symbolism and mythology. I will hereafter, with the same focus, discuss the ideology of the brilliant poet Lord Byron and his ironic epic *Don Juan* in relation to, and as a counterpart to, the ideology of Wordsworth. As the ideology of Wordsworth has had a central standing in literary theory throughout the twentieth century, his work will function as the thesis while the ideology of Byron will be his antithesis. I will thus argue how both ideologies function as a side of the same coin within the framework making up a synthesis. This synthesis functions within an infinitely expanding framework that widens with every new piece of information that contributes to a deeper understanding of the dynamic of the synthesis. It similarly expands with information on additional ideologies that provide counter arguments to function within the framework. This discussion will then culminate into a question. I have determined that the concept is expanding, but in which direction? In the more empirical perspective, the canon of works consists solely on the poetry of six male poets, but within the framework of this conception there is space for a wider range of literature. This includes additional genres, works and writers. I will in this case focus on the inclusion of women poets with a primary emphasis on the placement of the ideology of Mary Robinson within the literary framework of Romanticism.

Chapter 1

The Evolution of the Concept of Romanticism

As the focus on the internecine nature of literary periods is essential to understand the dynamic landscape of the literary scene, the focus of this paper will be on the Romantic Movement, as it is a powerful example of a literary scene characterised by sharp cultural conflict and historical differences. The case of the meaning of Romanticism as a concept has gathered much attention in recent times because the classic definitions of the concept seem to be too immobile to alterations of canon when provided with evidence for the need to do so. Jerome McGann called for a radical rethinking of the concept in 1996 in his renowned essay "Rethinking Romanticism" where he argues that the known generalisation of the concept based on a presupposed canon that already anticipates the core of the phenomenon does not accommodate fully the vast array of possibilities that truly lies within the meaning of the word. This line of thought, has in recent decades opened up for a debate on a more open meaning of the concept, as the literary critic Seamus Perry has mentioned "The difficulty is not just knowing what it really means, but knowing even *how to go about deciding* what it really means" (Perry, '*A Companion to Romanticism'*, p. 3). The dominant perspective until recent times has been the mentioned generalisation of the concept where one presupposes a canon through a return to the already known Romantics and then one defines a concept based on their similarities. What McGann here suggests with his radical rethinking, is to no longer try to define the period, but instead to explore and map the endless possibilities of the concept.

In order to open up for the possibility of such an exploration, Perry clarifies that one needs to resign one's claims of history and start a new without the boundaries of a presupposed canon, and instead "begin with a pure concept of 'Romanticism', a Platonic Idea, quite free of any empirical basis, and then let that concept determine your choice of canonical texts" (Perry, p. 3). In this way, the Romantic canon is no longer fixed on the works of an already anticipated set of known authors, but it is open to gradual development when presented with new evidence which calls for a change in emphases or an expansion of canon, as Perry also believes to be an important focus point "The canon of works may always be changed, with new works added, or emphases changed, for all kinds of reasons (we should not expect a general rule there); and the new evidence offered by the reformed canon will, in turn, alter the concept subsuming that canon; and vice versa" (Perry, p. 4). There is therefore an interest in a rethinking of the concept, as the concept of Romanticism needs to be able to accommodate a mutable canon of works.

Jerome McGann's essay is, along with being a call for a rethinking of the concept, a critique of the comparative literary critic Rene Wellek's notion from 1949 of a unified concept of Romanticism based on the similarities of the poets across the borders of Europe. In his essay "The Concept of Romanticism in Literary History" Wellek convincingly attempts to define Romanticism based on three central criteria, which he believed the Romantic canon of works have in common across Europe "imagination for the view of poetry, nature for the view of the world, and symbol and myth for poetic style"

(Wellek, p. 193). He places his focus on English Romanticism and goes on to describe in detail the outlook of the English Romantic poets within the elements of nature, imagination and symbol with the purpose of convincing the reader that the common traits of the poets are similar enough within these three criteria that one can define the very concept of Romanticism as one European movement. He does acknowledge differences "between various romantic movements, differences of emphasis and distribution of elements, differences in the pace of development, in the individualities of the great writers" (Wellek, p. 204), but even with these vast differences he believes the romantic views of nature, imagination and symbol to be coherent and mutual enough to create a complete definition of the concept.

Wellek's criteria became, as mentioned, a cornerstone in Romantic research after the Second World War. McGann intervened with *The Romantic Ideology* in 1983 which he claims helped to “stimulate what has become a vigorous and widespread discussion of the issues” (McGann, p. 161). In both his mentioned works, McGann criticises Wellek as he states that “it still seems to me: first, that Wellek’s position flattens out the rough terrain of the cultural formation(s) we call romanticism; and second, that Wellek’s position fails to map the phenomena comprehensively because it is a specialised view derived from a Kantian/Coleridgian line of thought” (McGann, p. 161-62). This means that in the period where Wellek’s definition dominated romantic research, critics interpreted romantic works within the frame of a permanently fixed ideology. Wellek’s definition of British Romanticism consists of a canon including only the works of the renowned male romantics of his time Wordsworth,

Coleridge, Blake, Keats, Shelley and to a lesser extent Byron. He therefore presumes a canon of the works of a set of known Romantics and defines the concept based on their similarities. The Romantic phenomenon, in this view, therefore becomes fixed on a specific set of qualities and elements that is not open to the addition of new works or gradual changes in emphasis as Perry and McGann have argued that it must always be in order to revise itself and mutate.

In light of the historical limits of Wellek's framework, McGann proposes, as mentioned, an alternative view that recognizes the boundaries of the concept and helps "one toward possible reimaginations of romanticism – to think beyond the conceptual framework of Wellek's synthetic theory" (McGann, p. 162). The understanding of the concept will then open up to the possibility of additional genres, themes, elements, happenings as well as additional writers who might be considered 'Romantic'. This casts light on an ongoing gradual process of a new Romantic canon of works as well as a general understanding of the concept that is less certain on its full meaning as it changes and mutates with every new group of literary participants who present evidence for an alternation of the understanding of the concept.

In addition to the rethinking of an expanding Romantic canon, there is also the question of a revival of certain previously considered Romantic poets that fall short under the definition of the Romanticism presented by Wellek, such as the famous poet Lord Byron. Many of the known Romantic writers may indeed fit Wellek's criteria, but in his efforts of generalising the concept to fit the central standing of Wordsworth and Coleridge, Byron's claim to a place as an important Romantic writer became more and more obsolete, or as McGann formulates it, “it is a theoretical and ideological fate” (McGann, p. 162). According to Wellek, Byron “does not share the romantic conception of imagination” (Wellek, p. 200), and he “does not share the fundamental rejection of the eighteenth-century cosmology nor the feeling of continuity and basic at-homeness in the universe of the great romantic poets” (Wellek, p. 200). Wellek does not hide the fact that his definition does not fit very well with the works of Byron, and therefore, as his framework became paramount, Byron’s deviation from the consensus of the concept was almost a complete reality.

The understanding presented by Wellek leaves itself permanently open to critique of the exclusion of certain known Romantic writers who do not fit the framework. This is especially problematic in the case of Byron, as McGann also notes “A Byronic vantage on the issue of romanticism immediately puts in question Wellek's imagination/nature/symbol tercet" (McGann, p. 162). Very little of Wellek's criteria matches Byron's writing style and outlook on the concept, as further explained by McGann " 'Imagination' is explicitly *not* Byron's view of the sources of poetry, 'nature' is hardly his 'view of the world' (Byron is distinctly a cosmopolitan writer), and his style is predominantly rhetorical and conversational rather than symbolic or mystic (McGann, p. 162). Thus, as Perry also mentions, Wellek's fixed framework leaves itself open to the critique of exclusion. Following this same line of thought, other Romantic writers may also deviate from Wellek's definition of the concept. If Romanticism is based on the Romantic poets seeing nature as their view of the world, then Blake also deviates from the norm. He, like Byron, does not take nature, as his view of the world, but since he shares the rejection of the eighteenth century cosmology and the feeling of continuity which Wellek clarifies that Byron does not, Blake's deviances seem to be overlooked. As McGann also clarifies, a deeper examination of the particular romantic writers individual outlook on nature, imagination and symbol will uncover significant differences. This means that the Romantic landscape is too dynamic and interchangeable to be generalized under a fixed framework and instead needs to be clarified under a more open understanding that can accommodate these differences.

The rise and rise of Blake, is in part because of a growing tendency to place idealism as central in the definition of the concept of Romanticism throughout the twentieth century. As naturalism became central to the definition of the concept, as Perry suggests, also did the conception of the introverted poetic genius living within the absentmindedly remoteness of his own consciousness sharing his innermost private thoughts in a state of solitude. Perry alludes to a saying by the British literary critic Lascelles Abercrombie from 1926 when he states that "romanticism is marked by '*a tendency away from actuality*" (Perry, P. 7) which fits well with the outline of "Imagination for the view of the world" by Wellek. This is, according to Perry, the dominant definition of Romanticism in 1926, which Wellek then further builds on in 1949.

Following this notion in an attempt to further define the concept, the literary critic Thomas McFarland critiques in 1987 Wellek's three criteria of, on the one hand, not encompassing "enough of Romanticism's characteristics to give us a reliable feeling of the contour of that sensibility, and on the other hand, the number three is still too large to claim unification" (McFarland, p. 13-14). Like Wellek,

McFarland tries to define the concept in a critique to a classic essay by the philosopher Arthur Lovejoy who states that "the word 'romantic' has come to mean so many things that, by itself, it means nothing" (Lovejoy, p. 66). Lovejoy argues that since there were several romantic movements across Europe that alluded to the concept in different ways, the meaning of the word, in itself, suffers from ambiguity. Wellek's answer to this was, as mentioned, to sum up their similarities and reduce the determinants of the concept to be based on the three criteria of imagination, nature and symbol.

In his critique, McFarland does not define the concept the same way as Wellek, who bases it on the writer's similarities, instead McFarland seems to claim unification despite their differences. He explains this notion by comparing Romantic understandings to sorts of trees, such as if one understanding is an 'oak' it is different from a 'linden' but they are both called trees, and therefore Lovejoy's different understandings can be generalised within the same concept. But, nonetheless, McFarland generalises the concept based on the same line of known Romantic authors and therefore he falls victim to the same illusion of a fixed ideology. In his attempt at encompassing a wider range of the characteristics of the concept, he identifies fifteen 'hallmarks' that, according to him, generalise Romanticism more adequately. The hallmarks consist of the classic elements of 'external nature', 'imagination' and 'a profound commitment to symbol', and then he further adds elements that, as Perry also claims, seem actually contradictory, such as 'a preoccupation with dreams' which stands in opposition to the classic element of "external nature" as well as 'a longing for the infinite' in opposition to a 'love of the particular'. In this light, Perry refers to Lovejoy, as he claims that "once a concept-label comes to cover several contradictory things, it risks losing its usefulness altogether" (Perry, p. 4). Thus, to sum up, even though McFarland operates with a wider range of elements, his unification falls victim to the same presupposed narrative as Wellek's, which results in a permanently fixed ideology. These elements, at the same time, contradict each other which puts at risk the meaning of the word altogether.

It is at this point illuminating to return to the history of the concept in order to recognise possible reimaginations that will further the perspective of a dynamic and mutable ideology that is open to a change in emphasis and an expansion of canon. A line of thought that might unflatten the rough terrain of the cultural formations of Romanticism is recognizing the stern internal conflicts that shaped the cultural philosophy from within, as McGann eloquently describes it "A romantic ethos achieved dominance through sharp cultural conflict; indeed, some of the fiercest engagements were internecine – the civil wars of the romantic movement itself "(McGann, p. 161). One thing which Wellek and McFarland seem to gloss over too lightly in their efforts of a distinct unification of the concept is the political and cultural context of the internally personal and working relationships of the Romantic writers. The poets who are classified today as 'Romantic' seemed very different in their own time, and many of them worked together and drew inspiration from each other as well as opposed each other both politically and culturally, as David Perkins also states in his work "On the whole, they disliked each other at least as much as they were friendly and admiring" (Perkins, p. 88). This consideration creates a more dynamic landscape that accommodates the differences and internal struggles of the Romantic writers who all had different outlooks on the uses and meanings of the Romantic elements and partly therefore they of course expressed themselves in different ways. But, why then, and how, did these different writers all come to be classified under the same label? And why is it important to think beyond this framework?

To answer this question, it is, as mentioned, illuminating to cast light on the history of the term 'Romanticism' itself. Wellek agrees with this sentiment, as he in 1949 described the sequential history of events in English Romanticism with the ambition of coherently classifying the term based on the similarities of the poets in response to Lovejoy's criticism of the term having become meaningless. My own ambition, however, is to locate differences and to further an understanding on the political and cultural struggles of the same poets as well as of additional poets and thereby follow up on McGann's notion of an open understanding of Romanticism.

To better understand the complexity of the term, an important point to recognize, with relation to British Romantic poetry, is that the word is a "posthumous invention" (Perry, p. 4) to borrow a phrase from Perry. The poets did not recognize themselves as 'Romantic', mostly because the word had a different meaning in their own time. Unsurprisingly, the term originates from the word 'Romance', and as Perry further describes, according to the Oxford dictionary the word 'Romantic' is from the early seventeenth century and means "either strictly, as a point of artistic classification, or more loosely, having the kind of qualities normally thought to characterize romance – 'Improbable; false', 'Fanciful; full of wild scenery' (Perry, p. 5). Wellek, in this case, also stresses that none of the English Romantic poets recognized themselves as Romanticists or show any awareness of the term in relation to their own work. However, Perry here highlights that Coleridge has tendencies toward a positive attitude to romantic literature. But, as Perry further exemplifies, in the mid-nineteenth century the Oxford dictionary listed the word 'Romantic' as being a word "which is wild, impracticable, and yet contains something which captivates the fancy' (Perry, p. 5). This is therefore the understanding which captivated the word at the time, which is why these writers whom we now consider Romantic did not consider themselves under the same label.

In the late eighteenth century, the term 'Romanticism' therefore did not classify a literary movement. Instead, the poets were categorized by contemporary critics into different literary "schools". Wordsworth, Coleridge and Southey became known as the poets of the "Lake

School"; the "Demonic" or "Satanic" school most prominently included "Byron and Shelley" and the "Cockney School" included "Hunt, Keats and Reynolds". In this case, a similarity between the poets is the negative feeling most of them shared toward their respective classifications. According to Perkins, the first person to combine the schools and classify them as "The Romantic School" was the French philosopher and critic Hippolyte Taine who generalised the concept in accordance with the philosophy of especially the Lake School in 1863. It is possible here, as Perkins speculates, that Taine was influenced by the notion of the "Spirit of the Age", though primarily he bases his classification on the French model of Romanticism.

Perkins' speculations are reasonable because in Romantic England, in the late eighteenth and early nineteenth century there was in fact a historical sense of change which transcended into the literary scene and shaped the writing of the poets. This is referred to as “The Spirit of the Age” and stems primarily from the French Revolution, or as Perkins states “more exactly, the extent to which this event preoccupied thought and emotion” (Perkins, p. 94). The English writer and literary critic William Hazlitt described it in his work from 1818 entitled *Lectures on the English Poets* as “a time of promise, a renewal of the world, and of letters; and the Deucalions, who were to perform this feat of regeneration, were the present poet-laureat (Southey) and the two authors of the Lyrical Ballads” (Hazlitt, p 180). The English Romantic writers became in this sense known as ‘dissenters’ of traditional norms, specifically the writers of the Lake School, were given this classification by the renowned critic Francis Jeffrey. According to Perkins, a group consisting of Scott, Byron, Wordsworth, Southey and

Coleridge later became united by the critic John Wilson as poets bound together representing the exalting spirit "of the same eventful age" (Perkins, p. 96). The grouping, at this time, is yet to receive a name and is classified roughly as radicals catering to the spirit produced by the common soul and thought related to the French Revolution.

The relationship between political history and literature became fundamental in a powerful way at this time because of the impact the revolution had on the literary scene and as a result then how the literary scene influenced the revolution. For Hazlitt, as the writer David Duff has argued, the French Revolution was more than just the central political event of the time, it also "formed the model ultimately for its most characteristic literary achievements, notably the 'poetical experiments' of its greatest poet, William Wordsworth" (Duff, 'A Companion to

Romanticism' p. 24). The idea that Britain experienced a literary revolution in parallel with the political revolution became publicly announced in 1816 by the English critic Leigh Hunt as he established Wordsworth, Southey, Coleridge and Byron as the established school of the revolution as well as Shelley, Keats and Reynolds as newcomers. Of this established 'first generation', Wordsworth experienced the revolution at first hand, but, as Duff specifies, all the known Romantic poets participated in the revolution either by journalistic writing or through fiction, drama or poetry.

The French Revolution continued to remain central to the British Romantic Poet's entire sense of the historical framework of their time. This is partly because the great varieties of English responses to the revolution in France led to intense political changes in Britain. This further resulted in a 'pamphlet war' which produced several controversies on fundamental political issues which, as argued by Duff "forms a key part of the intellectual background to English Romanticism" (Duff, p. 25). Of the established school of poetry, the first generation poets lived to regret their radical involvement in the revolution. They all shifted to more conservative positions in their later years to the dissatisfaction of the next generation. Especially Byron would denounce them as deserters of the rightful ideals of humanity. Perkins here convincingly sums up the literary revolution by referring to the 1814 *Critical Review*

The last half-century has produced, said the *Critical Review*, 'as great a revolution in the world of fiction as of fact. Within that time established customs have been set aside, grave opinions derided, and the bounds of poetic license extended beyond the limits of ordinary vision. Lord Byron is one of the mighty spirits who lead the revolt (Perkins, p. 95).

As Wordsworth and Coleridge eventually would become noblemen of the British government in their efforts of fighting the revolution, Byron opposed all forms of ruling classes over the common man.

As previously mentioned, these clear and distinctive differences in the Romantic writers make the Romantic landscape too dynamic to be defined on a fixed set of simple criteria. Especially in the case of Byron, Wellek's classification, as further noted, opens itself up to serious critique, because, even though Byron does not fit Wellek's criteria, it is extremely problematic to undermine his historic significance to the Romantic movement and ultimately to the concept of Romanticism. It is therefore important to realise that these classifications only work to give a practical overview of a field of study. The generalisations presented by critics over time change as the time change, as Perkins also argues in his presentation of shifting critical views of which none prove more correct than the others. This is because, as Perkins further states, the objects to be classified are heterogeneous. This means that critics must be selective and adopt a fixed point of view and therefore "in the process of being formed, classifications cease adequately to represent the past" (Perkins, p. 111). Thus, as times change, critics adopt new outlooks on life and therefore draw new lines in the process of forming these classifications, which are formed through presupposed agendas making them lose credibility. This is why the outcome has been multiple different classifications where none are more correct than the others. Instead, by altering the view from beginning with a canon based on a fixed concept to a less empirical standpoint which begins with an idea of Romanticism that gradually governs the choice of canon when new evidence presents itself. Then these very same critics will be able to contribute to a free flowing, ever changing and mutable landscape that can accommodate these differences.

Following this line of thought, a way to look beyond the forming of classifications based on presupposed frameworks is to locate significant historical and political similarities and differences in the literary scene during the Romantic period. A powerful example of this is the interpersonal relationship between two of the era's greatest poets William Wordsworth and Lord Byron. In the following, I will then analyse the two poet's major works *The Prelude* and *Don Juan* in an effort to better understand the internecine relationships of the Romantic scene and thereby contribute to the dynamic landscape of the concept of Romanticism. I will connect the two writers and their classic works both on a personal level and on a literary level. This is to prove just how different the literary works of the Romantic Movement can be and yet still remain as part of the dynamic framework. Wellek is definitely very much in the right when considering that Wordsworth falls in line with the traditional conception of Romanticism and that Byron does not, but that does not mean that they can't both be considered 'Romantic' on equal terms.

Chapter 2

William Wordsworth and *The Prelude* – The Educated Mind

In the case of Wordsworth, he and Coleridge arguably pioneered the literary revolution through their common work *Lyrical Ballads* from 1798. The two poets had an extraordinarily productive working relationship beginning in July 1797, which is, according to the British biographer Duncan Wu, "when the Wordsworths had moved from Racedown Lodge in Dorset to Alfoxden House, a few miles from Nether Stowey" (Wu, p. 1). During this time, Coleridge must have told Wordsworth about his plan for *The Recluse*, which in Coleridge's mind was to be "the poem that would herald the millennium" and which he would later describe as "the first and *only* true philosophical poem in existence"

(Wu, p. 2). The project, which Coleridge with confidence had bestowed upon Wordsworth, was dropped temporarily for *Lyrical Ballads,* which contributed economically to the Wordsworths trip to Germany, which they believed to be the intellectual centre of Europe. It was therefore the ideal location for the composition of the great philosophical poem of the age. Wordsworth continued on his project, but the location of the German city 'Goslar' was disappointing and the philosophical aspect of the project proved distinct from his main talents. As Wu also clarifies, Wordsworth found little inspiration in the German city and therefore he found himself one day writing in one of his notebooks,

Was it for this

That one, the fairest of all rivers, loved

To blend his murmurs with my nurse's song,

And from his alder shades and rocky falls,
And from his fords and shallows, sent a voice
To intertwine my dreams? (Book I, Line 269-274)

This moment of despair therefore caused the beginning of Wordsworth's ultimate masterpiece, his autobiographical work *The Prelude.* It is not the philosophical epic that was promised to Coleridge, but an autobiographical work in blank verse which allowed Wordsworth's creative energies to flow much more freely.

The Prelude was intended to be the prologue to *The Recluse,* which in theory was to consist of three parts. He worked on the epic his whole life, but never completed it. Wordsworth managed to compose or nearly compose four different versions of *The Prelude* during his lifetime. The first version was composed in 1798-99 and is called *The Two-Part Prelude* and contains the first two books on his life. On completion of the two-part volume, Wordsworth returned to write *The Recluse,* but the philosophical aspect resulted in much self-doubt and he eventually dropped the project to once again focus on a five-book volume of *The Prelude*. He never completed a five-book volume, but his intentions to do so, can be spotted in a letter he sent to Francis Wrangham in early 1804 "At present I am engaged in a poem on my own earlier life which will take five parts or books to complete, three of which are nearly finished (Wu, p. 13). In the work on his own life, Wordsworth quickly became uneasy on the fact that he had skipped the two important years between 1789 and 91, which are notable for his time in France during the early days of the revolution. He therefore decided that five books were inadequate "to express everything he had to say about the development of the imagination that prepared to compose *The Recluse*" (Wu, p. 14). He therefore dropped the five-book version, and started work on *The Thirteen-book Prelude.* He completed the work in 1805, but would not publish it until the completion of *The Recluse.* He kept working on *The Prelude* until his death in 1850. He never gave the poem a title, and it was unknown to the public until the final version was published in fourteen books three months after his death by his widow Mary Wordsworth. The thirteen-book version, which Wordsworth finished by the age of 35, was later edited by the literary scholar Ernest De Selincourt and published in 1926.

The resurrected version of 1805, I believe, is the clearest version of Wordsworth's philosophy at the moment of composition. In comparison, the posthumous version was altered and rewritten multiple times during the following years to fit his transition to a more conservative attitude to life. I will therefore primarily refer to *The Thirteen-book Prelude* in my analysis. I will, though, acknowledge all versions of the epic and refer to them when relevant.

The Prelude is considered to be Wordsworth's masterpiece. It is of great importance as it is one of the most insightful poetic works on the personal process within the mind of the poet as he undergoes the spiritual journey within his own memory. A primary reason for Wordsworth's central standing in Wellek and McFarland's classifications of Romanticism is because of his poetry's literary reflection of the romantic mood of the age. The poem's emphasis reflects the romantic mood, which is what historians refer to as the reaction to the neoclassical age of reason. The writers of this age preached scientific and philosophic enlightenment as if the laws of the universe were to be recognized and identified and the human race would then flourish in a rationalised and predictable world. This is because they thought of themselves as rising up from centuries of ignorance into a new and enlightened age rationalised by reason and science. Romanticism, with *The Prelude* as a central work, is in this sense, the disillusionment with the Enlightenment's way of seeing the world.

The Enlightenment was in itself a reaction to its predecessing centuries which it condemned as ages of darkness and mental oppression. It was a time of rational liberation, which moved on into an age of rationality and systemisation of thought. This is, according to the British author Peter Kitson, best demonstrated in the project of the *Encyclopédie* on which a number of different philosophies collaborated to collect and systemize all thought "Generally, there was an attempt to systematize and codify nature and society" (Kitson, *ACTR*, p.

35-36). The collection included Newton's laws of motion and Locke's delineation of the faculties of the mind. It was primarily English thinkers such as Locke and Newton who originated the ideas of the Enlightenment which were based on the notion that all knowledge was restricted only to what could be observed and identified through the senses. For Wordsworth and Coleridge though, it was more the empiricist philosophies of David Hartley in his work *Observations on Man* from 1749 which influenced their ideas. Hartley proposed a notion by which external objects create sensations in the mind of the recipient and thus creating the foundation for ideas, as Kitson explains "through the process of association we arrive at complex knowledge" (Kitson, p. 37). As further noted by Kitson, such ideas were influential as Wordsworth and Coleridge employed these associanist aesthetics as a method for understanding “the mind’s interaction with nature” (Kitson, p. 37).

When relating these notions to *The Prelude,* Wordsworth builds on the ideas of the ‘associanist aesthetics’ in order to create something new, as Kitson further speculates “there is something new, perhaps, in Wordsworth’s obsessive exploration of the psychology of his own self in his autobiographical poem *The Prelude”* (Kitson, p. 37). Indeed, as also hailed by the literary critic Jonathan Wordsworth “It is the great epic of human consciousness “(JW, *ACTR*, p. 179). Wordsworth in *The Prelude* takes as his subject ‘the human mind’. This is a theme that is, at this time, wholly modern and sees no direct comparison to earlier works. Wordsworth saw his epic as an extension, or even a replacement, of earlier great epics, measuring his own position in relation to the great works, most notably John

Milton's famous classic *Paradise Lost*. Milton saw his own epic as replacing Homer and Virgil, which is a sequence in which Wordsworth saw himself as the next step in the narrative. He notes that whilst Milton's self-stated purpose is to "assert Eternal Providence, / And justifie the wayes of God to men" (*Paradise Lost*, Book I, l. 25-26), he has chosen to look inward and has chosen his own imagination as the subject of his epic. Jonathan Wordsworth presents a convincing example of this claim when he notes Wordsworth's passage on the works of his predecessors in relation to his own theme in book III of *The Thirteen-book Prelude*

Of genius, power,

Creation and divinity itself

I have been speaking, got my theme has been

What passed within me! Not of outward things

Done visibly for other minds – words, signs,

Symbols, or actions – but of my own heart

Have I been speaking, and my youthful mind. (Book III, l. 171-176)

Wordsworth, in these lines, directly places himself in relation to his predecessors by claiming that they have written of 'outward things / Done visibly for other minds' while he has looked within himself and found 'genius, power, / Creation and divinity itself'. Thus, Wordsworth makes a powerful claim on the poem as a reflection of his own sense of his position and ability as a poet as he matures over the course of his life.

Wordsworth continues to build on the theme of the human mind, by returning to his own childhood memories and wondering how they effect and contribute to his matured sense of the world. *The Prelude,* therefore, in extension, contains the theme of learning and growing through experiences and then maturing through reflecting on these experiences. An example of this can be spotted in the earliest version of *The Prelude* in two books, with a return to the previously mentioned passage *Was it for this* which is "Wordsworth with no sources but the memory, imagination and speculative power of his own mind" (JW, p. 181). Through a rethinking of the 1799 poem, Wordsworth "defined for himself a link between childhood imaginative experience and adult creativity" (JW, p. 182)

Tragic facts

Of rural history that impressed my mind

With images to which in following years

Far other feelings were attached – with forms

That yet exist with independent life,

And, like their archetypes, know no decay.

There are in our existence spots of time

That with distinct pre-eminence retain

A fructifying vitue, whence, depressed

By trivial occupations and the round

Of ordinary intercourse, our minds –

Especially the imaginative power –

Are nourished and invisibly repaired (Book I, l. 279-94)

The 'associanist aesthetics' inspired by Hartley are here described. Wordsworth applies the concept in the poem as a reaction to tragic incidences, which then creates images in the mind of the recipient. They are images from childhood or in the recent past which are then reflected upon in the mind “becoming the focus of new imaginative feelings, such as the child could not have had” (JW, P. 183). The entire work therefore centres on the imagination of the poet shown through reflection on the effects of distant and recent extraordinarily emotional memories on his matured state of mind.

The concept of the imagination for Wordsworth draws heavily on the theories of Hartley which Wordsworth in *The Prelude* uniquely applies in relation to his own mind. Wordsworth thus applies his own perception to Hartley’s theories, as Wellek also notes “Wordsworth cannot be explained entirely in Hartley’s terms;” (Wellek, p. 194). Hartley believed, as mentioned, in the associanist theory of which external objects create impressions in the human mind which then form images and pictures in the mind through the association of thoughts. Therefore, according to Hartley, the mind passively echoes the external sphere, but for Wordsworth the imagination is a creative power which actively and creatively alters the external world. The mind of the poet is then analogous to the divine as it, like a divine power, creates and adds to nature; in other words "Imagination is thus an organ of knowledge which transforms objects, sees through them" (Wellek, p. 194-95). *The Prelude,* in relation, is a spiritual autobiography of the poet envisioning past memories in order to imagine the external objects which originated these previously felt emotions. The poet thereby actively alters the nature of reality through the creative powers of the mind. The creative power therefore becomes a protagonist in Wordsworth's rendering of the human mind, as Kitson also notes "Wordsworth makes the creative imagination the hero of spiritual autobiography in *The Prelude.* It is akin to the creative powers of nature and is 'reason in her most exalted mood" (Kitson, p. 39). As the human mind aligns with the divine, the poet perceives the concept of reason in “her most exalted mood” (*The Prelude,* Book XIV, l. 192), meaning that the poet “sees into the life of things” (Tintern Abbey, l. 50) and through the creative power visualise the divine.

In connection to the concept of imagination, for Wordsworth, the aspect of nature is an individualistic metaphysical element influencing the human mind in the form of a language of systemised symbols of natural forms. The everlasting divinity of the surrounding landscape, the soothing waters, the crags, the hills, all the beauteous forms exist with independent life in the infinite and interconnected romantic universe. In other words, he considered nature as a divine spirit pervading all the natural objects of the external world, as also elegantly described by Wellek “nature is animated, alive, filled with God or the Spirit of the World; it is mysteriously present, it gives a discipline of fear and ministry of pleasure" (Wellek, p. 197). He then systemises these objects as a metaphorical vehicle in his poetry, because he believed in the enriching influence of the spirit of nature to the human mind. Nature is both a source of joy in times of despair and an educational and moral influence to the mind of man. A primary ambition he has with his literature, and especially with *The Prelude*, is to educate his readers on the interconnection between nature and the human mind in relation to the elevating effects of the spirit on humans who open themselves up to the divinity of the creative powers of nature.

In particular books I and II of *The Prelude* primarily deals with educating the human mind through the moral teachings of the benevolent spirit of nature. The first book initiates with a literal journey back from the city of London to his beloved home in the countryside of the Vale of Grasmere located in the Lake District. He immediately feels a sense of spiritual freedom elevating his creativity that has previously been clouded by the nuisances of society. Removed from civilisation, Wordsworth describes how he, during his childhood, would be outdoors as much as possible, at all times of the year, so to absorb all the education the spirit of nature had for him. He emphasises the importance of this aspect through colourful portrayals of personal childhood memories "In Part II, as in Part I, we are offered vivid personal memories, intensified within the mind, because they are associated with particular landscapes" (JW, p. 185). This is because he considers openness to the moral teachings of the natural world being of great importance in the development of the child.

He clarifies this aspect further in book II where he portrays his childhood through adolescence and young adulthood. The young poet feels the interconnectedness of all things and becomes increasingly aware and appreciative of the beauty of nature. He appreciates his imaginative power and ability to consciously depict his early memories as a way to absorb the teachings of nature, and in doing so he describes maternal love as the origin and source to the imaginative power.

Blest the babe

Nursed in his mother's arms, the babe who sleeps

Upon his mother's breast, who when his soul

Claims manifest kindred with an earthly soul

Does gather passion from his mother's eye

Such feelings pass into his torpid life

Like an awakening breeze, and hence his mind,
Even in the first trial of its powers,
Is prompt and watchful (Book II, l. 269-77)

The tender love of the human mother to her infant child thereby originates the connection between nature and the mind of the child, as also described by Jonathan Wordsworth "it is the gravitational pull of nature (personalized in the mother's love) that makes the infant part of the world in which he lives" (JW, p. 186). The feelings of love from the mother fill the mind of the infant and develop in it the creative power, as also further argued by Jonathan Wordsworth "we are to see the child both as the credible human infant, and, symbolically, as the poet in embryo" (JW, p. 186). Thus, the effect of the mother goes beyond simple awareness of the interconnectedness of nature, it also creates the ability to use it as a source of moral learning and creative design.

In Wordsworth's conception, nature is an omnipotent spiritual entity interconnected in all things, sharing its knowledge with the human mind from the state of infancy through maternal love into adulthood by way of a connection between man and the natural world. This process is the source of the creative power fuelling the imaginary powers of the poet. Wellek gives a good example of a portrayal of the oneness by Wordsworth in the Simplon Pass passage where he describes how the rocks, the crags and the streams "Were all like workings of one mind, the features / Of the same face, blossoms upon one tree, Characters of the great apocalyps, The types and symbols of Eternity (Book VI, l. 568-571). Wordsworth's primary ambition with his poetry is to teach this knowledge for the common man to connect with the one spirit the way he did himself. He presents the oneness of all things to the reader in the form of a system of symbols. The natural forms are systemised in a symbolic language which expresses the eternal oneness of the world as presented in the mind of the poet through the imaginary power.

Following this, it is clear that Wordsworth "does stress imagery in his theory and is by no means indifferent to mythology" (Wellek, p. 201) and his style "is not without pervading symbols" (Wellek, p. 201). In relation to *The Prelude,* it narrates several literal journeys, such as the mentioned voyage to Grasmere in book I, as well as the crossing of the Alps in book VI and the ascent of Snowdon in the final book, which function as the elevating landscape of natural forms systemised in a symbolic language expressing to the reader the connection between the oneness of all things and the mind of man. In the 'Ascent of Snowdon' passage at the climax of the poem, Wordsworth describes how "The Moon stood naked in the Heavens, at height / Immense above my head, and on the shore / I found myself of a huge sea of mist, / Which meek and silent, rested at my feet: (*The Thirteen-book Prelude,* Book XIII, l. 41-44). When glancing upon the majestic landscape from the peak of the mountain he senses the spirit of nature "it appear'd to me / The perfect image of a mighty Mind, Of one that feeds upon infinity, / That is exalted by an underpresence, The sense of God, or whatsoe'er is dim / Or vast in its own being; (Book XIII, l. 68-73). Through powerful imagery of the sublime as seen from the summit of the mountain, Wordsworth continues to portray the magnificent effect of the spirit as an all-encompassing entity on the human mind, so that "even the grossest minds must see and hear / cannot chuse but feel" (Book XII, l. 83-84). The educated mind however, has the ability to visualise and understand the complexity of the universe as "a genuine counterpart / And Brother of the glorious faculty / Which higher minds bear with them as their own; This is the very spirit in which they deal / With all the objects of the universe" (Book XIII, l. 88-92). Thus through vivid imagery and symbolised language Wordsworth expresses the elevated sensation of the tutored mind.

In light of all this, Wordsworth clearly falls smoothly in line with Wellek's imagination/nature/symbol tercet. It is therefore understandable why Wordsworth became so central to 20th century critical thinking. But, considering the mentioned understanding of a concept of Romanticism able to accommodate a pure idea that is free of any empirical basis, then Wellek's tercet only makes up one side of the coin. Literary classifications can be useful for practical reasons, as Perkins also proclaims “literary classifications are at best practical conveniences, tools of exposition, helpful for certain jobs” (Perkins, p. 112). A fixed idea is therefore practical, and so, we should not dispense of terms such as imagination, nature and symbol, which McGann has also eloquently specifies, they are “primary philological data of the originary historical efforts to forge romantic experiences of the world” (McGann, p. 164). What is important to clarify in this regard is “the heuristic and constructivist character of those terms and the ideas they generate and pursue” (McGann, p. 165). McGann here correctly specifies that they are dialogical terms as the specific concepts of imagination, nature, symbol and myth are deployed individually by the romantic writers within defined conceptual frameworks. As shown above, Wordsworth himself tries to define the concepts of imagination and nature as he places them within the romantic discourse to fit his personal philosophy. The same is true with for example Coleridge and Byron and their personal philosophies of the same terms. We can therefore "speak of different (romantic) 'theories' of nature or imagination, and we can separate these different theories from each other" (McGann, p. 165). It is therefore possible to define Romanticism based on Wellek's criteria, but it is based on too fixed an ideology to outline the full meaning of the concept.

Following this, a more dynamic outlook on the Romantic scene is essential to understand that these different theories of Romanticism cannot be defined in simple terms. If Romanticism is then understood and treated as an, to borrow a word from McGann, aesthetic economy instead of a prescriptive economy, meaning as a "dynamic scene of evolving tensions and relationships, as in a family"

(McGann, p. 165) then it is not possible to systemize these theories. This is because each individual writer had a unique philosophy of Romanticism which led to internal tensions based on ideological conflicts and historical discrepancies. This is reflected in their literature, as also summed up by McGann "Romantic poetry, in short, constructs a theatre for the conflicts and interactions of the ideologies of romanticism" (McGann, p. 165). An aesthetic economy therefore refers to the less empirical understanding of the concept that takes into account the dynamic scene of a vast array of different writers with different ideologies that are built up based on different theories. The understanding of Romanticism thus becomes more dynamic because one can place these theories from each other and classify them accordingly and from there build an understanding of Romanticism that can accommodate these different theories as all being a part of the same concept. A prescriptive economy however, such as the one presented by Wellek, refers to the understanding with a presupposed agenda of how the essence of the concept is supposed to look like. In this sense, one have to fit the ideologies that match the dominating understanding of the concept while the misfits, such as for example Byron, are left behind. This is because the understanding is simply too narrow to fit all of them.

In this paper, I focus on Romanticism as an aesthetic economy. This means that each Romantic writer has his or her own personal ideology of Romanticism, and each of these personal ideologies goes into a larger framework. This framework is called the Romantic discourse. The Romantic discourse, in this sense, means that every individual writer inspired and got inspired by other writers, who had also developed their own personal ideologies of Romanticism. This makes the romantic scene a dynamic scene. As shown above, Wordsworth had his own personal ideology, his own idea of what 'imagination' is and what 'nature' is and what part these elements play in the larger framework of Romanticism. Coleridge and Byron for example, also had their own ideologies of Romanticism, their own values and theories, their own views of the world. It is when these ideologies start to conflict with each other that one gets internal tensions and conflicts on which ideologies best fit the framework of Romanticism. As McGann then explains, these ideologies can be studied and categorised, but it is wrong to leave any of them out or place any of them more centrally than others, because they all work within the same framework.

Chapter 3

Lord Byron and *Don Juan* – Romantic Irony

Especially the ideologies of Wordsworth and Byron are in conflict with each other. Byron is what the German romanticist Friedrich Schlegel in the beginning of the 19th century formulated as a Romantic ironist. In contrast to Wordsworth's philosophy of the elevated mind of the poet in alignment with the divine spirit of nature, the Romantic ironist has to recognize the limits of his own finite comprehension of a world which he sees as fundamentally chaotic. The renowned scholar Anne K. Mellor explains in her book *Romantic Irony* that "Romantic irony is a way of thinking about the world that embraces change and process for their own sake" (Mellor, p. 4). The Romantic ironist, in this sense, sees the world as an unpredictable realm where "No order, no far goal of time, ordained by God or right reason, determines the progression of human or natural events" (Mellor, p. 4). The chaos is dynamic and productively creates new forms, but "insofar as these forms are static and finite, they are inevitably overwhelmed by and reabsorbed into the process of life" (Mellor, p. 4). Mellor further compares the chaos to pure energy flowing in 'force-fields'. This energy appears as material objects but they are understood more precisely as "momentary conjunctions of differently charged forces" (Mellor, p. 4). The forces are in motion, but they are unpredictable because chaos has neither direction nor purpose.

Furthering this, Anne Mellor states that Romantic irony is both a philosophical conception of the world and an artistic program. This philosophical concept of course refers to the mentioned conception of the world as chaotic.

However, the artist who shares this conception plays what Mellor refers to as a "dual role" (Mellor, p. 14). The artist must embrace a sustainable art form that can fully express this chaotic world of never-ending creation and de-creation. The Romantic ironist must at the same time initiate his writing with both a sceptic and enthusiastic mind. First he must acknowledge his own limitations as a human being with a finite consciousness as well as the limitations of his man-made creations. Having ironically acknowledged his own mortality and the fictiveness of his structural and mythological designs, he enthusiastically begins the next phase, which is the romantic phase of creatively creating new structural forms and mythological designs. As the Romantic ironist is as enthusiastic as he is sceptic "He is as much a romantic as an ironist" (Mellor, p. 5). The artist then, in a state of recognized humanity, creates a finite world in which he is the omnipotent power. In this world he can enthusiastically commit himself to the creative process of creating new forms. These new forms then die "to give way to new patterns" (Mellor, p. 5), and therefore they continuously both create and de-create themselves. This never-ending process then becomes, as thoughtfully expressed by Mellor "an analogue for life itself" (Mellor, p. 5). To sum up, Romantic irony is a perception upon the world as consisting of infinite and purposeless chaos. This perception is then expressed through a literary art-form that can accommodate this "ontological reality, this never-ending becoming" (Mellor, p. 4-5). Under this philosophical conception, the artist then must recognize his own consciousness as both finite and involved in this reality in order to balance the creative process in an aesthetic mode that simultaneously creates and de-creates itself.

The Romantic landscape is essentially a disputatious scene. This is reflected in both the private and public literature of the age. It is therefore possible through the study of private literature, such as letters, diaries and notebooks, to gain a detailed portrait of a dynamic scene. And together with the study of the cultural and historical disparities of their literary works it is possible to get deep insight into the interconnectedness of the movement. As mentioned, my ambition is to show just how different and conflicting the Romantic Movement can be while still functioning within the same framework, and I believe an excellent way to do this is to examine and compare Lord Byron's ironic masterpiece *Don Juan* with Wordsworth's spiritual autobiography *The Prelude*. *Don Juan* is precisely a poem which McGann himself has called the "Counterpart and antithesis to *The Prelude*" (McGann, 'Byron and Romanticism', p.

179). The two poems are both central works of Romanticism, as they both make up a side of the same coin. Byron's philosophy of the mortal poet as an ironic creator of finite forms in a never-ending circle of creation and de-creation is therefore equal to Wordsworth's notion of the elevated mind of the poet in harmony with the divine spirit of nature, as Mellor also further states "Romantic irony was as significant and important a way of thinking about the nature of thc univcrsc and thc artistic proccss for nineteenth century English writers as was that other great intellectual tendency of the age, natural supernaturalism" (Mellor, p. 5). Natural supernaturalism here refers to the work *Natural Supernaturalism* by Meyer Abrams in which he argues for the English and German poets of the age sharing a common theme of the mind of man in parallel with the divine spirit. But, as he fails to acknowledge the philosophy of Romantic irony, he is in reality only describing one part of Romanticism, and not the whole concept.

In light of this, it is clear that not all Romantic works share the natural philosophy of the progress of man into unity with the divine. In fact, it is to the contrary as Anne Mellor also further notes that "many central romantic works exhibit a structure that is deliberately open-ended and inconclusive" (Mellor, p. 6). Such a work is Byron's *Don Juan* as well as Coleridge's classic poem "The Rime of the Ancyent Marinere" from the mentioned common work with Wordsworth *Lyrical Ballads*. But the insistence on placing these anti-systematic works within an inadequate systematic structure has led to radically conflicting readings of major works. While focusing on the historical importance of Byron, McGann also agrees that it is very problematic to disperse of *Don Juan* as a major Romantic work simply because it does not fit a specific schematic framework, which he clarifies "The subject of Byron's late masterpiece *Don Juan* was set aside altogether *so far as the question of Byron's romanticism was concerned.* For while here one could see, very clearly, a panoramic (dis)play of 'romantic irony,' Byron's work pursued its ironies in an apparently unsystematic and nontheoretical way" (McGann, p. 63). It is therefore important to recognize these ideologies as separate from one another and place them in a larger and more dynamic framework that can accommodate their differences. Or, more specifically, place them within a framework that values these differences precisely because they deviate from the norm. This is because each located deviation from Wellek's synthesis provides a clearer picture of the placement and function of the respective Romantic ideologies within the Romantic discourse.

Like Wordsworth, Byron experimented with implementing autobiographical elements in his more mature works. But unlike Wordsworth who reflected back on his own life Byron deliberately created a fictive "self" that is detailed enough to be believable. Byron presented in his later years this fictive self as a mode of consciousness who embodies his personal ironic philosophy. The artist Lord Byron therefore consists of a real "self" and an "artistic self". In his writing, one can trace autobiographical tendencies to his own life, yet he presents these events through fictive characters that see the world through his eyes. Byron purposely shortened the distance between himself and his creations in an effort to realise his fictive universe, as Mellor also clarifies "Byron deliberately blurred the lines between his 'real' self and his 'artistic' self. More and more, he lived the role imagined for himself, a heroic balancing between enthusiastic commitment and sophisticated scepticism" (Mellor, p. 31). Byron therefore mirrors Wordsworth's achievement of instilling his personal philosophy within the Romantic discourse by implementing themes and elements based on experiences from his own life. Though Byron's characters are not necessarily real, they are often clearly based on reality. It is all often described by an ironic narrator whose disillusioned views Byron deliberately designed to reflect his own.

The ideology of Byron is a fascinating and complicated one. His later works embody his personal perspective of an infinite and ever-changing chaotic universe. In his celebrated poem *Childe Harold's Pilgrimage* released in four parts between 1812 and 1818 he describes the life and reflections of a young man grown weary of a structured life and therefore leaves on a pilgrimage to the unknown. In this endeavour he learns that knowledge of the limits of the human mind and the possibilities of life comes through experiencing the world. His pilgrimage is therefore “a process of becoming” (Mellor, p. 31), as Mellor states it. This pilgrimage thus animates Byron’s view of life as unpredictable and in constant motion. The same perception can be felt in his dramatic poem *Manfred* written before the fourth canto of *Childe Harold* in 1817. Manfred is a character who, like the poet-narrator of *Childe Harold*, learns that the human mind can never comprehend the infinite chaos. He is forced to recognise his own mortal limitations but unlike the poet-narrator of *Childe Harold* who accepts it as a possibility to learn of life, he reacts against this reality because he sees it as a source of sorrow. In both remarkable poems, Byron’s perspective of the universe as fundamentally chaotic shines through and both poems also represent the limits of human consciousness in a state of becoming. But, they only represent one half of Byron's ideology. It is not until *Don Juan* that he finds the ideal art form for his artistic programme.

A vital thing to note about *Don Juan* is that, unlike *The Prelude,* the poem was released volume by volume to its readers. He began the poem in July 1818 and continuously released the poem canto by canto until his death on 19 April 1824. Upon his death, Lord Byron was working on the seventeenth canto of Don Juan, which is left unfinished. This method allowed Byron to gradually alter his statements within the poem to fit the status quo of his relationship with his readers. According to the scholar Jane Stabler, Byron deliberately released the poem this way "so that consequent changes in Byron's relationship with the English public are foregrounded as a dynamic of the poem" (Stabler, *ACTR*, p. 247). This method also allowed him to gradually mature the sensations of Don Juan to fit his own expanding world vision. It is therefore important, in all readings of the poem, to clarify where we are in the history of the poem when discussing a specific canto.

To get a sense of why it is important to keep clear of where one is in the history of *Don Juan*, one must look at the details of the publications of the poem. Byron published the first two cantos anonymously in 1819. But, as mentioned by Stabler, due to the expensive production and pre-publication rumours, the poem was recognised instantly as a poem by Byron. The first five cantos became published by the English publisher John Murray. He had become Byron's trusted publisher after he had helped cement his name with the publishing of Byron's work in highly regarded and expensive editions. However, Murray came into strong disagreement with Byron on whether to publish

Don Juan in the versions envisioned by Byron. The first two cantos had a mixed reception by most reviewers who found it morally appalling. After the publication of the fifth canto, Murray withdrew himself which led Byron to seek alternative publishers and ultimately ended up publishing the next volumes under the imprint of John Hunt. The reviewers continuously critiqued his work to be morally outlandish, which led Byron to campaign against the English public whom he found too prudish. In this light, Stabler suggests that *Don Juan* therefore can be interpreted as "a series of skirmishes leading to outright confrontation with the sexually prudish, religiously orthodox and politically Tory parties in Engand" (Stabler, *ACTR*, p. 248). It seems therefore that, as Stabler also specifies, to its initial readers the details of publication play a part to the meaning of the poem.

It is in this light that the scholar Peter Cochran in 2009 compared *Don Juan* to *The Excursion* which is a long poem in nine parts by Wordsworth. Wordsworth did intend, as mentioned, *The Prelude* to be the first part of a three part philosophical epic called *The Recluse,* and in this case, *The Excursion* was intended to be the second part. Wordsworth published this work in 1814. Although it did not receive much praise, according to Cochran it draws a great contrast to *Don Juan.* Cochran refers to the literary critic Marilyn Butler who claims that Byron directly countered *The Excursion* with *Don Juan.* Butler argues that "*Don Juan* was conceived in poetic and ideological reaction to *The Excursion*" (Cochran, p. 208). In comparison: Wordsworth is solemn, Christian and conservative. *The Excursion* is at the same time "a succession of personal histories in one retired spot" (Cochran, p. 208) as well as it “celebrates the victory of England, a Christian and traditionalist society, over France and innovation” (Cochran, p. 208). Byron however, is comical, sceptical, extrovert and panoramic, as well as providing “ribald and anarchic” (Cochran, p. 208) commentary “on the restored monarchies, the Holy Alliance, and narrow, canting England” (Cochran, p. 208). Byron also directly proceeds on directly sharing his opinion on Wordsworth’s work in *Don Juan* by calling it “A drowsy frowzy poem,” (*Don Juan,* Canto III, s. 110, l. 7). Byron could not have directly countered *The Prelude* as it is a posthumous publication, and therefore Byron never read it, but with an age difference of almost twenty years, a comparison between *Don Juan* and *The Excursion* gives a good idea of the personal and political distance between the two poets.

The Prelude though, speaks to Wordsworth’s younger and less conservative self.

As Wordsworth initiated *The Prelude* in blank verse to allow his creative energies to flow more freely in an endeavour to philosophically reflect back on his own life, Byron searched for an art-form that could ironically distance his artistic self to his fictive creations in a manner so he "carefully balances a romantic enthusiasm against a sceptical conviction of human finitude" (Mellor, p. 42). Cochran argues that, while resident in Venice, Lord Kinnaird read John Hookham Frere's epic *Whistlecraft* to Lord Byron. Kinnaird thereafter asked Byron if he did not think it very clever and difficult to which Byron replied that he thought it clever but not very difficult. Frere's mock epic is in the rhyme scheme known as *ottava rima.* Byron could use this rhyme scheme for a "mingled narrative yarn, offering the possibility of a rapid sequence of decasyllabic *ababab* appositions before the concluding couplet enabled an undercutting of the previous six lines (Romantic irony in performance), or an audacious lead into the next stanza" (Stabler, p. 249). This allowed him to instigate each stanza with a rhyme scheme that culminates into an often comical rhyming couplet. As the omnipotent narrator, Byron is ironically aware of his constant comical breaks in the midst of the seriousness of the poem. This satirical rhyming scheme together with the poem's publication method provided Byron with the ideal artistic programmc to compose his ironic masterpiece.

For Byron, the form of the poem provided a perfect outlet to balance chaos and order, As Schlegel also states, it should be an "artfully ordered chaos" (Schlegel). The art-form's rhyme scheme in iambic pentameter provides the poem with a balanced outlet as it culminates in a comical couplet that is ideal for providing an ironic distance between himself and his fictive creations. This orderly sequence, together with an everlasting publication method released volume by volume representing a chaotic universe in constant motion, as also described by Mellor "a never-ending improvisation" (Mellor, p. 22) therefore creates an artistic programme that can balance chaos and order. As Mellor has further argued, to reach this programme Byron had to make a transition from the tragic view of *Manfred* to a more comical and ironic view and the "agent of that transition was human love" (Mellor, p. 38). Byron needed to be released from the horrible memories of his past loves Augusta Leigh and Annabella Millbank. Peter Cochran here has argued that it is this desire for forgetfulness which anchors two of his major works, which he wrote in the aftermath of his marriage with Annabella, *Childe Harold III* and *Manfred.* Cochran further discusses how Byron likely did not believe that his incestuous relationship with Augusta was troublesome for him. Rather to the contrary, it was a blessing during a tragic time that he desperately wished to forget. But, as Mellor describes in her work, it was his mistress Marianna Segati who persuaded him that he was still capable of living a life of love. This led to a series of experiences with various women, and the important thing to take from that is "Byron's remarkable capacity to repeat, with intriguing variations, the experiences that brought him the greatest personal pleasure" (Mellor, p. 39). It was therefore his ability to love which released him from the past and brought him back into the present. Thus he was able to transition from the tragic view of *Manfred* into a more enthusiastically ironic view in *Don Juan*.

Wordsworth, in this context, also had things he wished to forget. During his time in revolutionary France in the early 1790s Wordsworth fell in love with a French woman named Annette Vallon. She gave birth to his daughter Caroline, but due to financial problems he had to return to Britain. During the following years he was not allowed to visit his family because of the hostilities between the two countries. Though *The Prelude* concerns Wordsworth's past, he does not directly write about these powerful memories at all. But it is clear that it did affect him and laid grounds for much of his matured sense of self. Byron on the other hand, as Cochran also argues, seems to drop hints in his poetry in a state of denial about his extended family. Therefore, as Cochran further writes "Wordsworth does not disguise his own past guilt – he just doesn't write about it at all. Byron pretends that he is writing about it, but isn't" (Cochran, p. 209). Wordsworth seems to have dealt with his own past memories through reflecting on them in harmony with the spirit of nature while Byron needed to be reminded by his mistress Marianna Segati about his capability to love and be loved in order to transition mentally from his tragic past and into a more enthusiastic present state of mind.

The sense of time in *Don Juan* reflects Byron's view of a chaotic world in constant motion. The chaotic time line of the poem repeatedly shifts between past, present and future. The poem begins in the present tense with a dedication to the other writers in which Byron directly shares his mostly controversial opinions of their poetry. He then proceeds in Canto I with the narrator claiming "I want a hero" (Canto I, stanza, 1 l. 1), and that hero is the mythological legend Don Juan. Byron then shifts the poem into the past tense in order to dive into the life of Don Juan and gradually follow his experiences and maturity in the chaotic world. This narrative is then, as previously mentioned, disturbed by frequent ironic breaks into the present, as Mellor puts it, the poem is “Repeatedly passing from fictive past to authorial present and back again, “Mellor, p. 42). The poem further extends into “that far goal of future time, an unreachable eternity” (Mellor, p. 42). Byron ironically reflects on the finitude of human consciousness and the limits of human knowledge on philosophical matters such as time and death.

For me, I know naught; nothing I deny,

Admit, reject, contemn; and what know you,

Except perhaps that you were born to die?

And both may after all turn out untrue.

An age may come, Font of Eternity,

When nothing shall be either old or new.

Death, so call’d, is a thing which makes men weep,

And yet a third of life is pass’d in sleep. (Canto XIV, s, 3, l. 1-8)

Byron's ironic reflections therefore balance the inadequacies of human knowledge in a chaotic and restless universe where nothing is certain "everything moves, changes its shape, becomes something different" (Mellor, p. 42), and not even time itself you can trust to be linear.

The only constant in this ironic universe is that all human philosophy can be trusted to be uncertain. In the travels of Byron's mythological hero Don Juan, neither time nor space stands still. His travels start in England and Spain then proceeds to Greece, Turkey, Ismail and Russia before going back to England, undergoing several personal relationships along the way. In this unpredictable and restless universe, Don Juan's continuous breakage of love affairs and constant establishment of new ones represent the instability of human affairs, as

Mellor also argues "In a world that so clearly moves in and out of chaos, human relationships are no more stable than physical objects" (Mellor, p. 43). This constant change of love affairs parallels the philosophy of Romantic irony of continuous creation and de-creation, as each lost love makes way for a new one which means that all "acts of destruction make way for new births" (Mellor, p. 43). In this world then, every human relationship is unstable. Yet, the human community sustains a sense of stability in an everlasting circle of human instability. In the poem society values this process as exemplified by Mellor "The court of Catherine, always producing new lovers for its queen, and the high society of England, making and unmaking matches and heirs" (Mellor, p. 44) . Society thereby actively builds on the process by making it possible for its members "to engage in a never-ending process of self-creation, self-destruction, and self-transcendence" (Mellor, p. 44). This means that the human community envisioned by Byron in *Don Juan* embodies his chaotic perspective of life itself. It is restlessly dynamic in a constant process of creation and de-creation.

The poem's hero Don Juan, in this way embodies Lord Byron's philosophy of human maturity through experiencing the world. As Wordsworth believed in the elevation of the human mind through the spirit of nature, Byron believed that it was through experience that man would be able to better comprehend the possibilities of life. Byron insisted that the finitude of the human mind would never grasp the infinite chaos. As shown in book I and II of *The Prelude* the young poet learns through walks in the nature of the Lake District until it culminates in his matured sense of self in book XIII at the tip of Mount Snowdon as he feels the divine. In *Don Juan* as well as in *Childe Harold* the travels of the respective heroes provide a platform for gathering experience and thus knowledge in an effort to gain self-transcendence. But the heroes are presented before their own human limitations as they learn that their human consciousness can never fully grasp the infinite. Especially in *Manfred* the protagonist is forced to recognize the ironic distance between his finite human consciousness and the infinity of life. Unlike Manfred, though, who rebels against his human limitations and experiences only tragedy, the heroes of *Don Juan* and *Childe Harold* accept their human finitude as a part of a process for self-transcendence and thus experience a sense of deeper comprehension of the infinite chaos.

Byron's philosophy of maturity through cosmopolitan experience flows together with Wordsworth's natural philosophy. This is because maturity for Byron is partly obtained through meditations upon the scenery of the places visited. Byron shares with Wordsworth belief in the teachings of the natural world to the human mind. Wellek exemplifies this by referring to the third canto of *Childe Harold*:

I live not in myself, but I become

Portion of that around me; and to me,

High mountains are a feeling, (Canto III, S 72, L. 1-3)

And Byron continues:

Then stirs the feeling infinite, so felt

In solitude, where we are LEAST alone;

A truth, which through our being then doth melt,

And purifies from self; it is a tone,

The soul and source of music, which makes known

Eternal harmony, and sheds a charm,

Like to the fabled Cytherea's zone,

Binding all things with beauty; -'twould disarm

The spectre death, had he substantial power to harm. (Canto III, S 90, L. 1-9)

It is only so that Byron negates the idea that man, no matter how educated, can fully comprehend the infinite. Nature is to Byron simply one of many factors in the cosmopolitan teachings of the mind of man. Wellek's conception of nature as "an organic whole" (Wellek, p. 196) is therefore present in Byron, though only 'fitfully' as it is not a primary concern within his philosophy.

McGann, in relation, argues here the aforementioned point of nature hardly being Byron's view of the world as he is primarily a cosmopolitan writer. This is true, since for Byron the true educator in life is sensation. He identified himself more as a 'traveller' than a poet that necessarily belonged to any one place. Like his fictive heroes, Byron travelled through many different countries, which is partly why *Don Juan* and *Childe Harold's Pilgrimage* are considered as semi-autobiographical travelogues. Mellor argues here how the mental and physical movements of Childe Harold embody a statement made by Byron in a letter to Annabella Milbanke "The great object of life is Sensation – to feel that we exist – even though in pain – it is this 'craving void' which drives us to Gaming – to Battle – to Travel – to intemperate but keenly felt pursuits of every description whose principal attraction is the agitation inseparable from their accomplishment" (Mellor, p. 4), and therefore, he continues "I can't stagnate" (Mellor, p. 4). This commitment to the teachings of life is apparent both in his poetry and in life itself. In *Don Juan,* Byron exemplifies this philosophy through the travels of Don Juan and his many experiences with love. Man must fully participate in the offerings of life, he must merrily multiply, experience the greatest of pleasures in infinitely various ways in order to fully participate in life, as Byron writes “Man, being reasonable, must get drunk; / The best of life is but intoxication” (*Don Juan,* Canto II, s. 179, l. 1-2). During such meaningful experiences, they “experience a kind of self-transcendence – and expansion of human possibility, a widening of the senses and the spirit that is the closest they can come to divinity” (Mellor, p. 46). Thus, one should pursue such experiences of intoxication, of human love, one should make love, get drunk, wake up and experience it again in infinitely various ways in order to fully participate in life and experience self-transcendence.

Byron’s attitude towards the placement of the concept of nature within the frame of the Romantic discourse is thus different than Wordsworth's. However, their respective theories on the concept flow together as they both believed in the teachings of the natural world, but only 'fitfully' as Byron only saw it as one of many fragments of a chaotic world which is supposed to be explored and experienced by humans. According to Byron, the finite human mind will thus develop and mature through meaningful experiences of human love and intoxication since these experiences provide a deeper comprehension of the infinite chaos.

Another aspect of Romanticism where Byron stands apart from Wordsworth, as well as the other great writers listed in Wellek's synthesis is the concept of imagination. Wellek states specifically in his essay that Byron is a poet who "does *not* share the romantic conception of imagination" (Wellek, p. 200). But, in this understanding of Romanticism, there is no single conception of imagination. There is no longer a central ideology within the framework. The multiple ideologies of Romanticism are all placed on equal terms next to each other. They dynamically flow together in an endless process of constant alteration. The outline of the Romantic framework is much like the chaos described in the philosophy of Romantic irony. It is also an endless process. The Romantic discourse is in constant motion. It is a dynamic scene, like a natural field with high mountains, flowing rivers and trees with leaves blowing in the wind. Just like the organic world it develops and grows with every new piece of information being appreciated as a new seed that can be planted in the ground. All of these ideologies are placed within this framework like bowls of energy in dialectical synthesis with each other. They constantly interlink and flow together because of their common theories and understandings of the normative themes and elements within the Romantic framework, such as Wordsworth and Coleridge's common conception of Hartley's theories founding their ideas on the imagination, which creates a thesis. At the same time, this thesis also creates its antithesis. The energetic field is also fuelled on the contrasting ideas of Wordsworth's natural philosophy and Byron's irony both claiming an equal place within the larger framework. This antithesis, together with the thesis, then creates a synthesis, and with every new piece of information requiring change in emphasis or expansion of the canon of works, this process further builds on a broader synthesis. The Romantic framework is therefore infinite and in constant motion.

As mentioned, the Romantic Movement is characterised by sharp internal conflicts and cultural differences. And two

Romantic ideologies standing in direct contrast with each other fuelling the fire of the movement are the ideologies of Wordsworth and Byron. And, as mentioned, one element where they deviate the most and create the most conflict is with regards to their contrasting ideas of the concept of imagination. Wordsworth attacked the poetic diction of the neo-classical age of reason in the preface to his and Coleridge's 1800 edition of *Lyrical Ballads*. According to Wordsworth, the poet is an educator who believes that "all good poetry is the spontaneous overflow of powerful feelings" ('Preface', *Lyrical Ballads*, paragraph 6, l. 20-21). The poet is educated through nature and teaches his inner thoughts through the imaginative power, and thus the mind of the poet exceeds beyond the common man. The ideas of the preface, which underlay the extended philosophy of *The Prelude*, became an emblem of the Romantic rebellion in the intellectual war against the neo-classical regime. It is therefore apparent that these ideas were of great influence and importance. But, for Byron the views of Wordsworth and Coleridge laid grounds for serious limitations to human philosophy. According to Byron the individual cannot solely prescribe meaning to reality, as McGann also argues in his work *Don Juan in Context*, "For Byron, the person existed in context, and the interaction of the two developed the reality we call the human world" (McGann, p. 156). This means that the Romantic position is limited because to them the individual is the source to all reality and truth. This constricts all living processes in the real world because to Byron the real world keeps spinning and all external things will be there whether they are a part of the poet's world or not. The person therefore exists in context; the context does not exist in the person.

Following this, *Don Juan* is Byron's own personal attack on the ideas of Wordsworth and Coleridge as McGann similarly argues "the whole point of *Don Juan* was to attack the 'Romantic' position especially" (McGann, p. 156). McGann further elaborates on this "*Don Juan* is constantly trying to remind Byron's contemporaries, and us, that the meaning of events passes beyond human perception because the contexts of events are always larger than our awareness. Insisting upon the primacy of the imagination, we become less imaginative, more self-absorbed, Lake-locked" (McGann, p. 157). For Byron the other Romantics were therefore guilty of restricting the context of life to purely individual terms. Outward forms have their own importance to the world surrounding it whether or not the poet is aware of it. We therefore "do not have to depend solely upon our imaginations" (McGann, p. 157). The meaning of external objects is thus not necessarily created by the imagination as Byron illustrates in the first canto of *Don Juan* when the husband of Juan's first love 'Don Alfonso' finds Juan's shoes in his bedchamber and tries to decipher why they are there:

A pair of shoes! – what then? not much, if they
Are such as fit with ladies' feet, but these
(No one can tell how much I grieve to say)
Were masculine; to see them, and to seize,
Was but a moment's act. (Canto I, l. 181)

Don Alfonso had already imagined the context, but was unable to decipher the code without the shoes. The shoes therefore have their own meaning in a larger context in which Don Alfonso is a part of. Don Alfonso thus "imagined himself a cuckold, but reality made him one" (McGann, p. 158). This scene imagined by Don Alfonso is also imagined from the views of Alfonso's wife 'Donna Julia', as well as the chamber maid, Don Juan himself and the imagination of circumstance. Byron does this to challenge the Romantic view of one individual's imagination being stronger than others. In the scene he illustrates how one cannot be in complete control of a situation that is in reality determined by multiple contexts which all arrange the events differently. Byron then shows that "Imagination is part of the human world, not its defining idea" (McGann, p. 159). Thus, in *Don Juan* Byron opposes the idea of the imaginative power of the educated poet as an educator that can elevate the mind of man in parallel with the divine. Instead the imagination is equally in all things within the contexts of life.

For Byron men cannot live in an inward world before they live in a larger world. Reacting towards that larger world is one of the struggles of life. The imagination is one of those reactions men have developed in order to deal with the world. Byron therefore believed in the imagination as a tool for art-forms that could show the contexts of life, as McGann also further argues "For Byron, this often meant the construction of imaginative systems which exposed the fact, and importance, of context itself" (McGann, p. 159). The human imagination therefore is as valid a tool for man to expose the contexts of life in art as it is in the real world. As a Romantic ironist, Byron takes an ironic distance to his creations in *Don Juan* and exposes their limitations as human beings. The finite consciousness of man must therefore look to the imagination in order to visualise the possibilities of the chaotic world. Fictive art is therefore a tool for human kind to realise possibilities or contexts that is not perceivable in the real world. According to Mellor, this phenomenon may even realise imaginative art as being more in touch with the real world than reality is because "insofar as artistic fictions often endure as a lasting recognition of a human possibility not realized in the present world, their bonds with the abundant chaos of noumenal reality may be the stronger" (Mellor, p. 48). Mellor here further exemplifies how the poet-narrator declares his creation as being real:

Don Juan, who was real, or ideal, -
For both are much the same, since what men think
Exists when the once thinkers are less real
Than what they thought, for mind can never sink,
And 'gainst the body makes a strong appeal;
And yet 'tis very puzzling on the brink

Of what is call'd Eternity, to stare,

And know no more of what is here than there;-
(Canto X, S, 20, L. 1-9)

Byron portrays here how the limits of human consciousness restrict the mind of man to ever adequately imagine the infinite chaos. What is real and what is not real is therefore up to the perceiver. Fictive creations, such as Don Juan, are as real, if not more real, than the real world itself because they are products of the imagination which can recognise possibilities that is not possible to realise in the real world. But since art is a product of the finite mind, it ultimately proves inadequate to imagine the infinite.

Byron's position in the framework of Romanticism is a special one. On many accounts, he stands in direct opposition to the other known poets of the age as is also accounted for by McGann “He assumes an adversary relationship, and institutes a sharp critique of the sort of poetry he himself – as he well knew – had helped to advance“(McGann, p. 159). This is well recognised, but as McGann further explains, Byron’s critical position is difficult to synthesise because he, unlike the other known poets of the age, never wrote a piece of expository critical prose. Unlike the works of Wordsworth whose preface became a symbol for the poetry of the age, one must look with different eyes at the poetry of Byron. This is because it is in his poetry that he gave his most thorough clarification on his position within the framework. McGann further specifies, by referring to Byron’s *Reply to Blackwood’s* and his “answers” to Bowles, that Byron’s attitude toward imagination is actually very conservative. He praises writers of the Enlightenment, such as

Dryden and Pope because their “work exhibits what is for him the highest excellence of verse – moral strength and discrimination: ‘In my mind, the highest of all poetry is ethical poetry, as the highest of all earthly object must be moral truth’” (McGann, p. 160). As Wordsworth believed imagination to be the source of poetry, Byron simply believed it to be one of many tools at an author’s disposal. In the same manner, Byron further distanced himself by regarding imagination and creativity as separate things. Imagination was only creative in the sense that it was “the source of the poet's *inventio”* (McGann, p. 160). Creativity or invention was therefore also a tool. The purpose of the imagination was thus not to create, but to ironically present fictive settings that more clearly exposed the human world. Byron’s idea of imagination is therefore not the source of poetry. Instead it is a common instrument that can be used to better reveal the chaos so that human kind may better understand it.

Byron took a direct adversary role to the other writers. He made known his position by directly attacking the principal values of the other poets. This is most clearly visible in *Don Juan*. Mellor argues in this case, that *Don Juan* is dedicated to an attack on the ideology of Robert Southey as he embodies “a closed, retrogressive mind and ideology” (Mellor, p. 56). Southey was, at the time Byron met him, famous for being a very influential right wing politician and a writer of epic poetry. Byron saw him as a closedminded bigot who stood for values directly opposite his own. In *Don Juan*, Byron celebrates the growth of human consciousness through travel, openness, intoxication, tolerance and love and by doing so he places himself in opposition to “death, stasis, repetition, retrogradation, closed minds and systems, bigotry and sterility” (Mellor,

p. 55). The poem thus embodies Byron's philosophy and attacks the Romantic position by standing in clear contrast to the ideology of Southey who generally shared his conception of poetry with the Lake School.

The poem itself celebrates values that stand in opposition to the ideology of Southey, but Byron also directly addresses the lake poets in a dedication that was published posthumously. He directly mentions Southey, Wordsworth and Coleridge as well as Southey's predecessor as a Poet Laureate, Henry James Pye. But, the poet who Byron opposes the most is definitely Southey. This is because the dedication is partly a reaction to comments made by Southey in his preface to *A Vision of Judgement* where he attacks Byron by stating that his writing "is a sin, to the consequences of which no limits can be assigned" (Southey, *Preface*, p. 18). Byron took it personally, and presents Southey as a “dry bob” which is slang for coition without ejaculation. It refers to him as being poetically impotent.

You, Bob, are rather insolent, you know,

At being disappointed in your wish

To supersede all warblers here below,

And be the only blackbird in the dish.

And then you overstrain yourself, or so,

And tumble downward like the flying fish

Gasping on deck, because you soar too high,

Bob, And fall for lack of moisture quite a dry Bob. (Ded, s, 3. l. 1-8)

Southey represented the ‘sterility’ and ‘bigotry’ which Byron opposes in *Don Juan.* Thus, the poem stands, by Byron’s own account, as a direct dedication to the poetically sterile Robert

Southey. It represents Byron's Romantic-ironic vision of the growth of the human mind through love and creativity, which stands in contrast to the stasis of the closed minded systems which Southey represents.

The attributes of *Ottava Rima* work well with Byron's intentions of directly belittle the lake poets while still keeping an ironic distance and a humorous tone. He makes full use of the possibilities of the rhyme scheme, as Jane Stabler also argues "Byron exploits the way that rhyme may be both a visual and an aural experience" (Stabler, *ACTR*, p. 249). Byron forces the reader to twist the pronunciation of words in order for it to rhyme. And, synchronically his use of quotation from other works and double *entrendes* "insists on the multiple meanings of the same word, forcing the reader to acknowledge (if not step into) other contexts" (Stabler, P. 249). His use of rhetoric therefore makes the reader realize another dimension in the writing. He acknowledges the infinite contexts of the world in the very language of the verse of *Don Juan*. Unlike the lake poets, Byron's style is not primarily focused on symbolism. His style is mainly "rhetorical and conversational rather than symbolic or mythic" (McGann, p. 162), as McGann also argues in answer to the synthesis presented by Wellek.

Byron, as also argued by Stabler, follows in *Don Juan* the imperative of Wordsworth's Preface to *Lyrical Ballads* by bringing the language of poetry closer to "the language of men" (Wordsworth, 'Preface', p. 9, l. 20). They both abstain themselves from the use of certain common poetic expressions that were notoriously repeated by poets of the age of reason. Wordsworth states in his preface that the reader of his poetry must utterly reject the current canon of criticism in order to enjoy his writing.

In the same vein, Byron's rhetorical use of slang and puns such as "a dry Bob" was met with disgust by many readers, and not least by his own publisher John Murray. Both Murray and Byron's friend John Hubhouse "expected such discourse to be kept out of poetry" (Stabler, p. 250). This sense of prudishness is what *Don Juan* is battling against. The poem did, as previously mentioned, receive much criticism for its unorthodox approach which fuelled Byron's campaign against the prudish English public. His poem directly confronted the Tory parties, the religiously conventional as well as his peers. Both writers therefore confronted the canon of criticism in their own way.

In order to fully gather all this it is necessary with a return to Wellek's imagination, nature and symbol synthesis. It is clear that Wellek's triad falls closely in line with Wordsworth's ideology. It is however also clear that the ideology of Byron represents a different side to the concept of Romanticism. Traces of Wellek's synthesis can be traced in Byron's work, but as McGann also argues, what one finds are differences. Byron held strong opinions on all these matters, but he took an adversary relationship with the lake poets. Wellek's narrow set of criteria and presupposed agenda toward what falls within the framework of Romanticism therefore push Byron to the periphery of the concept. But, in a dialectic understanding, Byron's adversary role takes the form of an antithesis to the thesis of the lake poets. This creates a philosophical forum that can accommodate and appreciate a wider set of ideologies. Within this forum, they stand equal with their own respective conceptions of truth contributing to the dynamic of the framework. As the canon of critics present new knowledge the framework expands. This is because, as mentioned, each presented antithesis to the current thesis leads to a broader synthesis. This process is continuously generated in an upward progression of thought. But, what is this new knowledge which expands the framework and in which direction is it headed? This I will discuss further to gain a clearer view on the evolution of the concept of Romanticism and its expanding canon.

Chapter 4

The Direction of an Infinitely Expanding Canon

This section concerns the current question of where Romanticism is headed. What knowledge is it that ultimately expands the framework? To answer this question one must study the current canon of criticism. This is because the understanding has opened up for alternative approaches to literary critique. As empirical and descriptive approaches to the concept are increasingly declining new areas of canonicity are explored and mapped. This process has thus resulted in the inclusion of additional topics, elements, contexts and writers that are considered Romantic. One area that especially challenges the dominance of Wellek's synthesis is the increased emphasis on gender and feministic criticism and theory. This line of feminist thought seeks to include women writers as part of the Romantic canon on equal terms with the male poets of the age. The list of women includes names such as Jane Austen, Mary Shelley, Dorothy Wordsworth and Mary Robinson, but to include these writers it is necessary to reflect on how this addition alters the general understanding of the concept. How did women think about writing literature compared to men and how did they influence each other? How does the involvement of feminist critique in Romantic literature change the way it is read and understood? Feminist criticism is in this case an antithesis that has been generated into a synthesis through much reflection on these precise questions. My ambition with this section is thus to examine which extra dimensions this line of thought adds to the framework of Romanticism. My analysis will place primary focus on the influence of the famous Shakespearean actress and poet Mary Robinson. But a discussion on the specific influence of women studies is necessary to fully grasp the effects it has on the literary framework of Romanticism.

In order to recognise the influence of women poets it is important to study with attention on the history of feministic writing. Through such an analysis it quickly becomes clear that much of the Romantic landscape is influenced by women writers. The renowned scholar Stuart Curran argues in his essay from 1988 "Romantic Poetry: The I Altered" that women writers had in fifty years moved themselves from the margins of the literary world to its very centre. He argues that there were actually more women novelists than men and the theatre was also dominated by women artists. And within the realm of poetry women also, at least for a time, had more influence than men. It is therefore insufficient to have a Romantic canon that consists of only male poets. A succession of influential women poets came to prominence in the 1770's and 80's. Writers such as Anna Barbauld, Hannah More, Charlotte Smith, Mary Robinson, Anna Seward and Helen Maria Williams as well as many more who emulated them. They are according to Curran 'the missing link' because "their achieved and independent excellence intimating a radical reordering of existing social institutions" (Curran, p. 188). The women were followed by another generation of great female writers who challenge the synthesis of an exclusively male canon. They function as 'the second missing link' because they "published far into the Victorian period and it would appear more productively and influentially than any male Romantic contemporary, with the exemption of Leigh Hunt" (Curran, p. 188). The success of these women and the recognition they obtained thus attest to a gradual movement to a more central standing in the literary world during this period.

Considering this influence on the literary scene it is only fitting that they should gain an equal place within the literary canon of works. Only few of these women have earned much Romantic-era critical attention before the 1980's. Susan J. Wolfson clarifies in her essay "Romanticism and Gender" how Romantic-era has since been reinvigorated by gender studies. The dominance of male writing is thus being reconsidered to the advancement of a burgeoning female canon within the framework. Gender studies has even gone so far as questioning the validity of the label 'Romanticism' because it "describes affective, aesthetic and political issues central primarily to men's writing" (Wolfson, *ACTR,* p. 387) while it diminishes subjects related to women's writing such as "female heroism, female desire, domestic affections, home and family, community, female childhood and education, motherhood, and last but not least, women's careers, especially as writers, outside the home" (Wolfson, *ACTR,* p. 387). Gender criticism does not try to marginalise the established canon of male works; it only questions whether the label 'Romanticism' is able to fully describe the expanding canon of works.

In consequence of the increased focus on feminist and gender studies, the Romantic canon is expanding to include a more gender-based line of thought with a vast array of female writers contributing to the canon of works. Gender criticism has developed from feminist studies and it expands its knowledge to consider situating the male canon in relation to women's writing in a comparative analysis. This has contributed to a new outlook on the canon of works. As Wolfson also argues, Wordsworth's *The Prelude* and Byron's *Don Juan* tended to be central to the 'masculine tradition' without any further thought to the poet's very different relations with women. Gender criticism focuses on this area of the poet's tendency to stereotype 'feminine attitudes' that "interrupt, or perhaps even shape, these poems, as well as many others in the male canon" (Wolfson, *ACTR,* p. 387). Gender criticism reflects and adds to the established canon of criticism that focuses on the social structure of gender differences and breaks down the mediating distance between men and women in order to demystify and destabilise past stereotypes of feministic literature. The Romantic framework thus expands with a feministic and gender-based dimension that focuses on establishing common ground between male and female writing. This is made possible through an understanding of the concept that is free of an empirical basis, but instead lets the idea of the concept determine the choice of canonical works.

A feministic dimension to the Romantic canon is especially necessary when considering that the first great treatise in English feministic philosophy is written during the Romantic period. Mary Wollstonecraft's *A Vindication of the Rights of Woman* from 1792 is one of the founding texts of modern feministic thought. In an age where women were considered 'masculine' when expressing any rational line of thought and were often met with ridicule at the attempt, Wollstonecraft argued for equality between the sexes. She argues that it is beneficial for both genders to treat women as both reasonable and rational human beings deserving of a proper education instead of mere sensual people who are not able to contribute intellectually to society. According to Wolfson, it is one of the founding feministic texts because much of the discussion continues as a critique of both literary and cultural works by men. It includes criticism on literary texts such as Milton's *Paradise Lost* and Rousseau's *Emile* while also focusing on cultural texts on issues such as the gendered vocabulary of the social evaluations of a patriarchal society.

In her criticism of a gendered vocabulary Wollstonecraft also takes a gender critical approach. As men have often proudly condescended women as being weak and sensual creatures, Wollstonecraft accuses some of the most highly regarded male poets and thinkers of being sensual. As Wolfson also argues, she faults Milton of making contradictory arguments regarding sexual hierarchy and equality in *Paradise Lost* and Rousseau is criticised with making errors in reasoning that "arose from sensibility, and sensibility to their charms women are very ready to forgive When he should have reasoned he became impassioned" (Wollstonecraft, chapter V, section I, p. 58, l. 1-3). Her argument is thus that if a woman can spot the lack of reason in men then reason is not solely a masculine quality. Wollstonecraft thus convincingly demystifies in 1792 the stereotype of women's lack of rational thought. Since the standard response to the idea of female rationality was generally hostile during the Romantic period, it is not surprising that the chronology of the Romantic canon developed into being dominated by men. But by focusing on multiple ideologies of Romanticism, instead of a central ideology constituting the centre of the concept, women writers are appreciated as an antithesis generating a broader synthesis. And through gender studies it is possible to gradually collect knowledge on the respective ideologies of these women and their placement within the framework as well as their individual contributions to the dynamic of the concept.

These women were, as Curran argues, the 'subtext' to Wollstonecraft's influential work. They created a core of female writers who successfully challenged the male canon of works and thus embodied her argument of women's ability of rational thought on equal terms with men. In the same vein, the famous artist Mary Robinson could in the 1790's characterise the literary landscape of the period as dominated by female authors and artists. Robinson, along with several other women intellectuals, greatly influenced the literary scene during the last decades of the eighteenth century. And as mentioned, they were followed by a second generation who unlike their male counterparts managed to transition into Victorian verse. As Curran also argues, their inheritance as poets is not the synthesis of the male dominated ‘big six’, but rather a generation of women poets who rose up against a patriarchal society. These women poets share many traits in their poetry with the male Romantic writers, as Curran further states “They wrote satires as well as sonnets, tragedies along with *vers de societé; a few even wrote epics*” (Curran, p. 189) and “some of the genres we associate most closely with British Romanticism, notably the revival of the sonnet and the creation of the metrical tale, were themselves strongly impelled by women poets” (Curran, p. 189). The respective ideologies of these women poets and the influence they had on both each other and the male poets will thus broaden the understanding of the concept.

As these women poets share many poetic modes with their male contemporaries, they are also so strikingly different as to suggest yet another dimension to the framework of Romanticism, or as Curran calls it “a terra incognita beneath our very feet" (Curran, p. 189). In contrast to Wordsworth's language of symbolism that elevates the human mind in alignment with the spirit of nature, women's Romantic poetry is more concentrated on the commonplace aspects of the natural world. This is because the poetry of women poets of course reflects their own natural world. As a woman's place in society was often that as a mother caring for her children in her private home and garden, it was often those surroundings that laid the foundation for verse. The distinctive aspect of this discipline is thus that it is concerned with minute objects found in the everyday. Instead of absorbing the oneness of the entire external world, distinguishing the character traits of particular objects becomes sufficient as an end in itself. This discipline has "the capacity to encode values, not just of culture but also of perspective" (Curran, p. 190). Curran further states "Its significance is quotidian" (Curran, p. 190), which means that the natural world experienced in women's poetry is not a spirit that aligns with the mind, but rather it exists for its own sake. The natural world is no longer combined into one by a benevolent spirit, the poetry tries to gather and discriminate between particular fragmented natural objects.

A visionary poet within the discipline of quotidian poetry is Mary Robinson. This genre is often associated with the poetry of the writers of the Victorian or of the Modernist movement. But Robinson's ability to portrait the real world in its most ordinary fashion during a time of war is powerful. Her writing, along with the literature of other women of the Romantic period such as Mary Mitford, Anna Barbauld and Charlotte Smith, suggest that Romantic writers pioneered the genre. Curran refers to Robinson's poem "January 1795" where she in 11 quatrains portrays the commonplace during wartime for all involved. She cunningly juxtaposes her references to the point where the context of war is barely visual. No matter one's occupation or rank in society "Poets, painters, and musicians; Lawyers, doctors, politicians" ("January, 1795, s, 9, l. 1-2) are as "gallant souls with empty purses" (s. 10, l. 1) and "Honest men who can't get places" (s 11, l. 1). They are all seeking fame and elevated positions in society in an endless universal pursuit of "mundane and amoral self-aggrandizement" (Curran, p. 191). And as Curran further exemplifies, Robinson's poem "Winkfield Plain; or, a Description of a Camp in the Year 1800" can be taken as an example of a pinpoint description of the actual world during war time.

Tents, *marquees*, and baggage-waggons;
Suttling houses, beer in flaggons;

Drums and trumpets, singing, firing;
Girls seducing, beaux admiring;
Country lasses gay and smiling,
City lads their hearts beguiling;
Dusty roads, and horses frisky,
Many an *Eton boy* in whisky,
Tax'd carts full of farmers' daughters;
Brutes condemn'd, and man who slaughters!

And she continues:

More of *war* than profit dreaming;
Martial sounds and braying asses,
Noise, that ev'ry noise surpasses!
All confusion, din and riot,
Nothing clean – and nothing quiet.

Robinson portrays the commonplace within the actuality of war, as Curran states "the quotidian is absolute" (Curran, p. 192). Her ability to place all citizens, no matter one's place in the hierarchy of society, within the same bracket as immersed in the actual of the surroundings captivates the reality of the time in piercing fashion.

As these women poets devoted much energy into distinguishing the particular of the everyday within the close quarters of the private sphere, it can be argued that they explored most vividly the extent of which the language of the quotidian could be incorporated in poetry. And thus, as Curran also argues, the real language of men is actually more so the language of women. It is thus arguable what should be associated with the label 'Romanticism'. Wordsworth's preface, Byron's rhetoric and Robinson's quotidian all suggest different conceptions of truth. It is therefore clear that the mentioned philosophical forum that is generated from this process not only opens itself up to an expansion in the canon of works, it also opens up for a gradual alteration of emphasis in relation to literary elements such as genre and themes associated with the concept.

Considering all this, it is clear that there is cause for much emphasis to be placed on gender-based philosophy which calls for an expansion of canon to include women poets along with an alteration of the existing canon to include the influence of gender studies. Another dimension that broadens the framework under such influence is the female perspective and impact on the understanding of poetic form in relation to their male contemporaries. A powerful example of this is the innovative use of rhyme and meter in Robinson's 1800 poetry collection *Lyrical Tales*. The title of the volume is inspired by Wordsworth and Coleridge's collection from 1798 *Lyrical Ballads*. But unlike *Lyrical Ballads*, many of Robinson's poems from *Lyrical Tales* had already appeared in the newspaper called *The Morning Post* and so she composed her poems to a very specific audience. The Scholar Daniel Robinson argues in his work *The Poetry of Mary Robinson: Form and Fame* from 2011 that this "is the major difference between Robinson's *Lyrical Tales* and Wordsworth's *Lyrical Ballads*" (Daniel Robinson, p. 216). Wordsworth's preface suggests that his collection aims for a much wider literary audience. Robinson seeks to stand out to her audience with her formal variety so much of the substance of her poems lies in the innovativeness of her formal style. As Wordsworth specifically seeks to "speak the language of men" and thus teach the common man from the elevated position of the genius poet, Robinson's poems "literally perform their artifice in the strangeness of their form" (Daniel Robinson, p. 217). The high variety and innovativeness of her formal choices thus speak volumes about her artistic deviance from her contemporaries.

Robinson's use of 'Lyrical' in her title is her acknowledgement of Wordsworth and Coleridge's formal innovativeness in *Lyrical Ballads*. However, as Daniel Robinson further argues, her borrowing of the title in a collection with more formal qualities than Wordsworth and Coleridge's own work insinuates that she "pits her own formal virtuosity against theirs" (Daniel Robinson, p. 217). Coleridge especially was interested in Robinson both as a poet and as a woman. He explicitly expressed interest in her formal style which can be seen in his comments on Robinson's poem "The Haunted Beach" where he states that the poem is lacking in substance but "the Metre – ay! that woman has an ear" (Coleridge, *Letters* I, p. 332). After reading the poem in *The Morning Post* he wanted to include it in Southey's *Annual Anthology*.

Coleridge was struck by the poem for several reasons, as Daniel Robinson also clarifies, its seaside setting, supernatural elements, its themes of guilt, crime, punishment combined with its wild imagery suggest strong resemblance with Coleridge's own famous poem "The Rime of the Ancyent Marinere". Robinson's poem "The Haunted Beach" tells of a lone fisherman who supposedly murders a "A Shipwreck'd Mariner". This is because the mariner after the wreckage on the beach lies murdered in the fisherman's hut "With ten wide gashes in his head". The fisherman is then haunted by "the spectre band" which is his drowned shipmates. The fisherman is afterwards ridden with guilt because of the murder and is therefore tied forever to the beach without any possibility of redemption. According to Coleridge, the poem's tale is not successful "because it does not relate an interesting story" (Daniel Robinson, p. 199). Coleridge states in his letter to Southey that the poem "wants tale and interest" (*Letters* I, p. 332), which means that the poem is lacking substance, but he finds the images "new and very distinct" (*Letters* I, p. 332). He also finds the poem's form and meter fascinating.

Robinson's poem "The Haunted Beach" consists in the version published in *Lyrical Tales* of nine lyrical stanzas with nine lines. Daniel Robinson argues that it is as difficult to rhyme as the Spenserian stanza, "but with shorter, and more incantatory, alternating lines of four and three stresses, with an augmented rhyme in the second and fourth lines" (Daniel Robinson, p. 220). Daniel Robinson further argues that the augmented rhyme is of particular importance because Coleridge found it to be especially significant to the form of the poem. Curran also argues in his essay "Mary Robinson's *Lyrical Tales in Context*" that Mary

Robinson usually eschew from simple ballad meter and instead employs innovative and complicated “stanzaic and sonic patterns” (Curran, p. 27). Coleridge’s interest in Robinson’s “fascinating metre” (*Letters* I, p. 332) is partly due to the efficiency of her augmented rhyme in creating a ‘haunting’ atmosphere. The metrics of each line is however absolutely necessary in creating the poem’s final form, as the stressed beats effectively create a dark musical undertone that fits with the poem’s obscure and mysterious narrative. This haunting atmosphere is immediately established in the poem’s first stanza

Upon a lonely desart Beach
Where the white foam was scatter’d,
A little shed uprear’d its head
Though lofty Barks were shatter’d.

The Sea-weeds gath'ring near the door,
A sombre path display'd;
And, all around, the deaf'ning roar,
Re-echo'd on the chalky shore,
By the green billows made.

The poem is clearly similar in both style and content to the mentioned poem "The Rime of the Ancyent Marinere" by Coleridge. Curran also argues that this fact is probably what attracted Coleridge in the first place. But as Daniel Robinson also notes as he refers to Curran, Robinson's ability to balance rhyme, meter and repetition in order to create such a haunting atmosphere to match the story's narrative surpasses "the capacity of Coleridge's ballad meter, however brilliantly employed, to assume complementary meaning" (Curran, p. 28). Thus, according to Curran, the meter applied by

Robinson matches the subject matter of her poem better than Coleridge's meter does in his poem.

It seems likely that Robinson, like Coleridge, is counting stressed beats instead of syllables. This is what Coleridge refers to when he comments on her 'ear". Coleridge saw in her a poetic voice capable of inspiring his own. And like Coleridge, Wordsworth also recognized the innovativeness of her verse in "The Haunted Beach" as he used her stanza for his own poem "The Solitude of Binnorie" which became published in *The Morning Post* in October 1800. Daniel Robinson mentions here that Coleridge took it upon himself to write a headnote to Wordsworth's poem in which he acknowledges Robinson's lines as a reminder to the readers of the "bewitching effect of that absolutely original stanza in the original Poem, and who call to mind that the invention of a metre has so widely diffused the name of Sappho, and almost constitutes the present celebrity of Alcæus" (Daniel Robinson, p. 221). Mary Robinson became known as "The English Sappho" in celebration of her first volume of poems in 1791. As Daniel Robinson also notes, Coleridge attributes Robinson with inventing a new meter and with its establishment it "promises fame to its creator in subsequent performances of that form by other poets" (Daniel Robinson, p. 222) and Coleridge's subsequent point is "that Robinson 'Thc English Sappho' has created a form that may become, like the original Sappho's, eponymous" (Daniel Robinson, p. 222). Thus, as Coleridge compares the eponymous form associated with the greek poet 'Sappho' he celebrates Robinson's meter as a new invention to the world of letters. This speaks volumes for Robinson's standing within the framework of the concept as a Romantic poet who has contributed with innovative poetic designs associated with the concept of Romanticism.

In a similar vein, Curran also argues in “Mary Robinson and the New Lyric” that it is more than metrics that are accountable for the effects of the poem. He further states that the essence of the matter of the poem lies within the timbres produced by her meter which can be spotted in for example “The Sea-weeds gath’ring near the door / A sombre path display’d (s. 1, l. 5-6) and “And then, above the haunted hut / The Curlews screaming hover’d;” (s. 5, l. 1-2). Robinson introduces the commonplace of the seashore, but in a few lines she turns it dark and mysterious. Curran argues that the verbal units that both drives and disrupts her other poem “January 1795” return “with an incumbent sense of a process that is alien, unchanging, and unstoppable – waving, craving” (Curran, p. 19). This process goes well with the subject matter of the poem because as Curran states “nature sports with human misery: stanza after stanza, year after year, those ‘green billows play’d’” (Curran, p. 19). Form and subject matter therefore comes together. Yet, as Curran further argues, it is the innovativeness of the form that has most to do with the success of the poem.

Coleridge clarifies in his preface to his poem “Christabel” in its 1816 publication that he had founded the poem on the principle of counting the accents in each line instead of the syllables. A year later in his publication of *Biographia Literaria* he stresses the qualities of new metres to which “the generous reader humours his voice and emphasis, with more indulgence to the author than attention to the meaning or quantity of the words” (Coleridge, Chapter XVI, p. 3, l. 11-12), which means that the meter urges readers to ‘hear’ the rhythm of the poem’s melody. As Daniel Robinson also argues, it then seems that Coleridge's praise of Mary Robinson's music stems from a combination of her inventive stanzas and accentual meter which suit the effect of the poem's subject matter which belongs to the genre of 'the gothic'. Both poets shared a mutual interest in the exploration of the unconscious through the mysterious qualities of the supernatural as Daniel Robinson states "both Robinson and Coleridge employ versification as a conscious fixing of the unconscious in and as form" (Daniel Robinson, p. 210). Robinson and Coleridge are thus connected as writers based on more than their innovative experimentation of form and meter; they both used their experimentations in a shared interest in the exploration of the unconscious through the dreamlike qualities of the supernatural.

Coleridge experiments with meter in many of his most classic poems such as

"Christabel", "Kubla Khan" and "The Rime of the Ancyent Marinere". As Daniel Robinson also mentions, the same process of experimentation can be spotted in many of Robinson's poems from *Lyrical Tales* as well as original poems such as "The Savage of Aveyron" and "The lady of the Black Tower". These poems clearly demonstrate that the two poets shared an aesthetic interest in the mysterious qualities of the supernatural. Even with such vivid experimentation, Robinson's poem "The Haunted Beach" is still one of her most original works. Both Wordsworth and Coleridge recognized the innovativeness of her poetry, yet Coleridge seems especially admiring of the way her technical mastery of poetic form suits the genre of the supernatural. The scholar Tim Fulford similarly argues that Coleridge appreciated Robinson's ability of "Suspending the reader's expectations of narrative sequence" (Fulford, p.

18) which is a technique Coleridge especially deemed vital in supernatural poetry. This is because, as Coleridge believed, it was through mastery of poetic form that the poet could create an atmosphere that for a moment could make the readers forget about their disbelief in the surreal which would make them lose themselves in the dark and mysterious atmosphere of the poetry. He is thus admiring Robinson's ability to make her readers listen to the sound of her beats in a temporary state of disbelief in reality.

With all this in mind, Robinson has earned her place as an equal to the great Romantic poets within the framework of Romanticism. In leaving her out of the frame, one ignores her original contributions to the Romantic Movement. Coleridge especially celebrates Robinson's "invention of a metre". Her innovative literary contributions would thus be associated as part of the Romantic canon along with her inclusion in it. Her productive working relationship with The Lake Poets through their common literary contributions to *The Morning Post* also speaks volumes about her accomplishments as a poet. Her position as chief correspondent for the newspaper's poetical department saw her contribute an extra ordinary amount of innovative poetry to the newspaper. Coleridge's comments on her abilities are thus appreciated as praise for a fellow poet on equal standing in the literary world. Daniel Robinson argues here that she would have thoroughly earned the gesture, "given her active participation in the professional and textual network around the creation and innovation of Romantic narrative form" (Daniel Robinson, p. 223). Thus her original contributions and cooperation with the Lake Poets around the time of the literary revolution in Britain suggest that she effectively and productively participated in the literary revolution on equal terms with the Lake Poets.

Mary Robinson's connection to the Lake Poets extends beyond professional cooperation. Robinson did not have much of a personal relationship with Wordsworth and Southey, but with Coleridge she enjoyed occasional social gatherings and free poetic exchange. During this exchange, Coleridge must have shared with her an early version of his poem "Kubla Khan" because she replied with a poem of her own entitled "Mrs. Robinson to the poet Coleridge" in which she publicly admires the masterful adaption of poetic form he displays in order to fully express the poetic imagination. In the same vein as Daniel Robinson, the scholar Heidi Thomson argues in her work *Coleridge and the Romantic Newspaper: The 'Morning Post' and the Road to Dejection* from 2016 that Coleridge shared with Robinson a mutual understanding which he did not find in any of his other peers. Thomson specifically clarifies this point as she writes "she understood what he wrote, and how he wrote, in a way no other contemporary did" (Thomson, p. 172). The two poet's internal understanding of supernatural poetry is therefore a valid reason as to why Robinson is arguably the first person to read Coleridge's masterpiece about sixteen years before its official publication in 1816.

Following this, Heidi Thomson also argues that the depths of Coleridge and Robinson's relationship go further beyond mutual understanding of each other's artistic abilities and interests. Despite a significant age difference Coleridge found comfort in her affections and praise at a rather difficult time in his life. According to Thomson, during this time Coleridge was in a state of despair because of his failing marriage and because he felt excluded by

Wordsworth in the newest publication of *Lyrical Ballads*. The exclusion of "Christabel" proved a traumatic experience for Coleridge which only got worse until he felt himself in a state of despair as it happened around the same time as his marriage deteriorated. As well as sharing her passion for ballad-inspired accentual meter with Coleridge, Robinson would also empathise with his separation which proved an invaluable comfort to him. During this time therefore Robinson was more than a valued fellow author, she was also a trusted friend who offered comfort to Coleridge. Her standing among the Lake Poets is thus as both an artist and as a woman who inspired and got inspired on both a professional level and on a personal level.

The poetic exchange between the two poets continued after Coleridge moved with his family to the city Keswick in July 1800 which effectively stopped the personal meetings between them. A few months later Robinson published a tribute to Coleridge's infant son entitled "Ode, Inscribed to the infant son of S.T. Coleridge" in which she, as Thomson also claims, celebrates Coleridge's artistic talents through the poetic connection between father and son. Both of Robinson's poems "Mrs. Robinson to the poet Coleridge" and "Ode, Inscribed to the infant son of S.T. Coleridge" thus directly celebrate the poetic genius of Coleridge. In both poems Robinson further confirms hcr familiarity with Coleridge's classic works of the supernatural such as "Kubla Khan". She praises Coleridge by not only showing a unique understanding of his poetry, but her poetic tributes also mirror the formal choice of his masterpiece. As Daniel Robinson also argues Robinson's "Ode" paints Derwent as the son of a poetic genius as he as the child is a metonym for the creative power.

SPIRIT OF LIGHT! Whose eye unfolds
The vast expanse of NATURE'S plan!
And from thy Eastern throne beholds,
The paths of the lorn trav'ller Man!
To thee I sing! Spirit of Light! to thee
Attune the varying strain of wood-wild harmony. (s. 1, l. 1-6.)

Robinson continuously alludes to Coleridge's son as 'The spirit of light' as he, as the son of genius, is a source of inspiration. She further alludes to the setting of the Lake District "Ye silent LAKES! That trembling hail / The cold breath of morning gale" (s. 3, l. 7-8) as an ideal setting for the son of genius to learn from and inspire his father. Robinson was at this time at the end of her remarkable career while Coleridge was just at the beginning of his and thus in this one of her final odes she pays tribute to the rising genius of Coleridge by alluding to the creative inspiration of fatherhood as well as mirroring the metrical variety of his classic masterpiece.

Mary Robinson's posthumously published poem "Mrs. Robinson to the poet Coleridge" is especially interesting because it provides a fierce indication on the depths of their affection and admiration for each other as well as their mutual understanding of poetry. The fact that Coleridge would share his masterpiece "Kubla Khan" with her sixteen years prior to its publication indicates that he thought a great deal of her. In addition, her poem reveals that she understood the supernatural elements of "Kubla Khan" in a way that none of his other peers did. In fact, as Daniel Robinson also argues it would take more than a century before the scholar John Livingstone Lowe would show a similar understanding of Coleridge's poetry "Robinson understood aspects of 'Kubla Khan' that no one else, at least in print, would begin to understand until John Livingstone Lowe's *The Road to Xanadu* in 1927" (Daniel Robinson, p. 199). She is thereby the first person to show that she understands "Kubla Khan" as a supernatural poem about the imagination in a way that would not be shown in a similar fashion for more than a century.

In "Mrs. Robinson to the poet Coleridge" Robinson directly positions herself as a sympathetic admirer and as an understanding fellow poet by alluding to the "sunny dome" and the "caves of ice". She does this in the same irregular metre as Coleridge which suggests that she shows her understanding of his poetry by mirroring it which Daniel Robinson also argues "she slyly winks at Coleridge by showing not only that she understands the matter of his "Kubla Khan" but its meter as well" (Daniel

Robinson, p. 228). Coleridge's poem features two masculine characters. One is called the Khan who is a powerful statesman and the other is a poetic genius. Both of these men are accompanied by a woman. The Khan Kubla is connected to "the woman wailing for her demon lover" and the poetic genius with the Abyssinian maid who is a symbol of the imaginative power. Her song can inspire the creative powers of the narrator himself. Tim Fulford argues here that Mary Robinson implies in "Mrs. Robinson to the poet Coleridge" that she associated herself with the inspirational Abyssinian maid

I'll mark thy sunny dome, and view

Thy Caves of Ice, thy fields of dew!

Thy ever-blooming mead, whose flow'r

Waves to the cold breath of the moonlight hour! (s. 2, l. 5-8)

Robinson thus refers to herself as a fellow poet who will mark his "sunny dome" and view his "Caves of Ice" which means that she offers herself as the Abyssinian maid to his poetic genius.

In addition to mirroring Coleridge's lyrical irregularity and thereby expressing her unique understanding of his poetry she takes on the challenge of using it to create her own song as Fulford also further claims "She shares the Abyssinian maid's song with Coleridge, and then gives him a song of her own inspired by it" (Fulford, p. 17). She thus creates her own innovative structure inspired by Coleridge's poem. She directly praises "Kubla Khan" as a poem of artistic inspiration.

With THEE I'll trace the circling bounds

Of thy NEW PARADISE extended;
And listen to the varying sounds
Of winds, and foamy torrents blended. (s. 1, l. 5-8)

By reading "Kubla Khan" she thus became inspired to develop her own form as Daniel Robinson also further argues Coleridge has opened a "new paradise" for aspiring poets to explore the endless possibilities of combining form and theme in order to create music.

Considering the poetic exchange between Coleridge and Robinson it is clear that they inspired and got inspired by each other. Their respective ideologies thus flow together adding to the dynamic of the framework. Robinson's original contributions to the construction of Romantic poetic form as well as her active participation in the social and textual network of Romantics during the period further cement her place as a Romantic poet. In relation to this, Daniel Robinson also points out that Coleridge himself commented that Robinson's innovative poetry should grant her "poetic longevity and legitimacy" (Daniel Robinson, p. 223). This all suggests the longevity of Mary Robinson as a Romantic poet within the framework of Romanticism, but she is in fact one of several women deserving of a place alongside the Lake poets. In the aftermath of McGann's theory the inclusion of gender studies has "reinvigorated" (Wolfson, p. 387) the concept as Wolfson also states. Wolfson further argues that during the dominance of Wellek's synthesis writers such as Mary Wollstonecraft and Jane Austen were infrequently read and studied as part of the Romantic concept. However today, the effects of gender studies have made it possible to include a wide range of female poets in the

Romantic canon. Duncan Wu's 2012 edition of *Romanticism: An Anthology* includes writers such as Anna Seward, Anna Letitia Barbauld, Hannah More, Charlotte Smith, Mary Robinson, Joanna Baillie, Dorothy Wordsworth and Felicia Hemans. As mentioned the inclusion of these women calls for a rethinking of traditional Romantic values because the male dominance has been challenged which means that a female perspective on central Romantic elements might alter the emphasis placed on them.

The Effects of a Dialectical Perspective

Considering all this it is clear that Wordsworth, Byron and Robinson represent different values while at the same time they each represent a respective side of the concept of Romanticism. Wordsworth's notion of the elevated poet in alignment with the spirit of nature, Byron's ironic philosophy of cosmopolitan sensation and Robinson's expression of the unconscious through the strangeness of her form as well as the genre of the quotidian all represent original poetic values developed during the literary revolution of the late eighteenth and early nineteenth century. Wellek's synthesis is thus too narrow as it only accommodates the common ideology of an already established canon. It only represents fragments of the past because it anticipates the concept in advance based on the similarities of a set of known male Romantics. Wellek's, and also McFarland's orderly viewpoints are therefore incomplete because they do not take into account the cultural context and the internal relationships between the writers. In the perspective offered by Wellek the concept of Romanticism thus solely consist of the ideologies of six male Romantics with the Lake Poets standing centrally on a permanently passive scene. As Perkins argues, such a constructed line of thinking does not offer a plausible perspective which can fully represent the past.

As an alternative to Wellek's constructed viewpoint, this paper has aimed to present a plausible perspective which steps beyond the limitations of theoretical forms. It has sought to present a dialectical viewpoint where the ideology of the Lake Poets no longer stands as central. In this perspective there is no single central ideology because they all stand as equals flowing together contributing to the dynamic of the concept. Byron takes an adversary role to the Lake Poets presenting his own conception of truth to the framework which means that his ideology takes the form of an antithesis to Wordsworth's thesis. This process creates a philosophical forum which generates a synthesis. Wordsworth's *The Prelude* and Byron's *Don Juan* are therefore two works that each represents a part of the concept. Wordsworth's *The Prelude* provides a thorough representation of Wordsworth's philosophy of the gradual education of the mind of man through reflection on the teachings of the divine spirit of nature. *The Prelude* similarly provides a good indication of Wordsworth's viewpoint on the Romantic elements of 'imagination, nature and symbol'. Wordsworth proves to fall in line with Wellek's criteria while Byron has alternative ideas on the uses of the same elements. Wellek's synthesis is therefore incomplete as it fails to accommodate the ideology of Byron. The mentioned dialectical perspective, on the other hand, is in fact able to accommodate the differing views of Byron as part of the concept because conflicting views are appreciated as contributing to the dynamic of the Romantic landscape.

A dialectical perspective precisely opens up for the introduction of new and conflicting information which provides a deeper understanding on the dynamic of the literary scene. It is, as mentioned, an energetic field where all of the ideologies stand in dialectical synthesis with each other. They constantly flow together on the basis of their common conceptions of the placement of normative Romantic values within the framework. The dynamic scene is also fuelled by information on conflicting views which take the form of antithesis within the philosophical forum which then generates a broader synthesis. This process thus results in a dynamic framework in constant motion that gradually expands its canon of works. It changes emphasis on certain theories and values related to the concept when new information presents itself. New areas of canonicity are thus explored and mapped which has resulted in the inclusion of additional writers, genres, contexts, elements and subjects to the canon of works.

One area that definitely expands the Romantic framework is the increased emphasis on the inclusion of feministic and gender-based criticism and theory to the canon of works. This line of theoretic thought seeks to include women poets as an equal part of the Romantic framework. Women writers transitioned during a span of fifty years from the periphery of the literary world to its very centre and actually dominated literary genres associated with

Romanticism. It is therefore clear that Wellek's male dominated representation of the past is incomplete. This point is especially clear when considering the visionary poetry of the brilliant female intellectual Mary Robinson. Her deep understanding on the combination of poetic form with the mysterious elements of the supernatural is especially praised by Samuel Taylor Coleridge. Her poem "The Haunted Beach" is a powerful example of her ability to create an innovative poetic form that creates a musical atmosphere that goes together with the supernatural elements of the poem. Her poetic exchange with Coleridge further proves her unique understanding of the supernatural elements of Coleridge's poetry. Her productive relationship with the Lake Poets testifies to her active participation in the poetic network during the literary revolution. She has therefore earned her place as an equal within the framework of Romanticism. The inclusion of

Robinson's innovative poetry within the Romantic framework thus calls for a complete reconsideration of emphasis placed on traditional Romantic values. Increased emphasis on gender theory has further broadened the framework with the inclusion of several other influential female writers whose original contributions have resulted in a complete reinvigoration of the concept. The dynamic landscape of Romanticism is thus infinitely expanding in a never-ending process of alteration.

Works Cited

Abrams, Meyer. *Natural Supernaturalism: Tradition and Revolution in Romantic Literature*. Norton, 1973.

Butler, Marilyn. Review of *Don Juan in Context* by Jerome McGann. *Essays in Criticism* 1978, pp. 52-60.

Byron, George Gordon. *Childe Harold's Pilgrimage*. Project Gutenberg. Retrieved May 29, 2017. http://www.gutenberg.org/files/5131/5131-h/5131-h.htm

- *Don Juan*. Project Gutenberg. Retrieved May 29, 2017. http://www.gutenberg.org/files/21700/21700-h/21700-h.htm
- *The Works of Lord Byron: Poetry Vol IV, edited by Ernest Hartley Coleridge.*

Project Gutenberg. Retrieved May 29, 2017. https://www.gutenberg.org/files/20158/20158-h/20158-h.htm

Cochran, Peter. *"Romanticism" – And Byron.* Cambridge Scholars Publishing, 2009.

Coleridge, Samuel Taylor. *Letters of Samuel Taylor Coleridge*, edited by Ernest Hartley Coleridge. Vol 1. Project Gutenberg. Retrieved May 28, 2017. http://www.gutenberg.org/files/44553/44553-h/44553-h.htm

- *The Complete Poetical Works of Samuel Taylor Coleridge Vol I and II*, edited by Ernest Hartley Coleridge. Project Gutenberg. Retrieved May 28, 2017. http://www.gutenberg.org/files/29090/29090-h/29090-h.htm

- *Biographia Literaria*. Project Gutenberg. Retrieved May 28, 2017. https://www.gutenberg.org/files/6081/6081-h/6081-h.htm

Curran, Stuart. "Romantic Poetry: The I Altered." *Romanticism and Feminism*, edited by Anne Mellor.

- "Mary Robinson and the New Lyric." *Women's Writing*. Vol 9, Nr. 1, 2002.
- "Mary Robinson's *Lyrical Tales* in Context." *Re-visioning Romanticism: British Women Writers, 1776-1837,* edited by Carol Shiner Wilson and Joel Haefner. University of Pennsylvania Press, 1994.

Fulford, Tim. "Mary Robinson and the Abyssinian Maid: Coleridge's muses and Feminist Criticism." *Romanticism on the Net* 13, 1999.

Gleckner, Robert, editor. *Romanticism: Points of View*. 2nd ed. Wayne State University Press, 1975.

- Lovejoy, Arthur. "On the Discrimination of Romanticisms." Robert Gleckner, pp. 66-81.
- Wellek, René. "The Concept of Romanticism in Literary History." Robert Gleckner, pp. 181-205.

Hartley, David. *Observations on Man: His Frame, His Duty, and His Expectations. In Two Parts.* 6th ed. Thomas Tegg and Son, 1834.

Hazlitt, William. *Lectures on the English Poets Delivered at the Surrey Institution*, edited by Alfred Rayney Waller and Ernest Rhys. Project Gutenberg. Retrived May 28, 2017, from http://www.gutenberg.org/cache/epub/16209/pg16209-images.html

- *The Spirit of the Age: Or Contemporary Portraits, 4ed.* Edited by W. Carew Hazlitt. George Bell and Sons, 1886.

Latané, David. Review of *Is Literary History Possible* by David Perkins. *South Atlantic Review*, Vol 57, No. 4, 1992, pp. 109-111.

McGann, Jerome. “Rethinking Romanticism”. *The Challenge of Periodization: Old Paradigms and New Perspectives*, edited by Lawrence Besserman, Garland Publishing, Inc, 1996, pp. 161-178.

- *Byron and Romanticism.* Cambridge University Press, 2002.
- *Don Juan in Context*. The University of Chicago Press, 1976.
- *The Romantic Ideology*. The University of Chicago Press, 1983.

Mellor, Anne. *English Romantic Irony*. Harvard University Press, 1980.

McFarland, Thomas. *Romantic Cruxes*. Oxford University Press, 1987.

Milton, John. *Paradise Lost.* Project Gutenberg. Retrieved May 28, 2017, from http://www.gutenberg.org/cache/epub/26/pg26.html

Perkins, David. *Is Literary History Possible?*. The John Hopkins University Press, 1992.

Robinson, Daniel. *The Poetry of Mary Robinson: Form and Fame*. Palgrave MacMillan, 2011.

Robinson, Mary. *Mary Robinson: Selected Poems, edited by Judith Pascoe*. Broadview Press, 1999.

Southey, Robert. “Preface” *A Vision of Judgement*. Longman, 1821.

Stillinger, Jack. *Multiple Authorsship and the Myth of Solitary Genius*. Oxford University Press, 1991.

Thomson, Heidi. *Coleridge and the Romantic Newspaper: The Morning Post and the Road to 'Dejection'*. Palgrave Macmillan, 2016.

Utara, Natarajan. *The Romantic Poets: A Guide to Criticism*. Blackwell, 2007.

Wollstonecraft, Mary. *A Vindication of the Rights of Woman with Strictures on Political and Moral Subjects*. Thomas and Andrews, 1792.

Wordsworth, William. *The Five-Book Prelude*, edited by Duncan Wu. Blackwell Publishers Ltd, 1997.

- *The Thirteen-Book Prelude*. Vol I., Cornell University Press, 1991.
- "Preface" *Lyrical Ballads: With Other Poems*. Vol I, 2nd ed. Biggs and Co, 1800.

Wordsworth, William and Samuel Taylor Coleridge. "Tintern Abbey", "The Rime of the Ancyent Marienere". *Lyrical Ballads: 1798-*

1802. Edited by Fiona Stafford, Oxford University Press, 2013.

Wu, Duncan, editor. *A Companion to Romanticism*, Blackwell Publishers Ltd, 1998.

- Duff, David. “From Revolution to Romanticism: The Historical Context to 1800”. Duncan Wu, pp. 23-34.
- Fay, Elizabeth. “Romanticism and Feminism”. Duncan Wu, pp. 397-401.
- Kitson, Peter. “Beyond the Enlightenment: The Philosophical, Scientific and Religious Inheritance”. Duncan Wu, pp. 35-47.
- Perry, Seamus. “Romanticism: The Brief History of a Concept”. Duncan Wu, pp. 3-11.
- Shaw, Philip. “Britain at War: The Historical Context”. Duncan Wu, pp. 48-60.

- Stabler, Jane. "George Gordon, Lord Byron, *Don Juan*". Duncan Wu, pp. 247-258.
- Wolfson, Susan. "Romanticism and Gender". Duncan WU, pp. 385-396
- Wordsworth, Jonathan. "William Wordsworth, *The Prelude*". Duncan Wu, pp. 179-190.

Wu, Duncan, editor. *Romanticism: An Anthology 4th ed.* Blackwell, 2012.